The Insider's Guide to the

Psychology Major

The Insider's Guide to the
Psychology Major

EVERYTHING YOU NEED TO KNOW ABOUT
THE DEGREE AND PROFESSION

AMIRA REZEC WEGENEK and WILLIAM BUSKIST

American Psychological Association • Washington, DC

Published by
American Psychological Association
750 First Street, NE
Washington, DC 20002
www.apa.org

To order
APA Order Department
P.O. Box 92984
Washington, DC 20090-2984
Tel: (800) 374-2721; Direct: (202) 336-5510
Fax: (202) 336-5502; TDD/TTY: (202) 336-6123
Online: www.apa.org/books/
E-mail: order@apa.org

In the U.K., Europe, Africa, and the Middle East, copies may be ordered from
American Psychological Association
3 Henrietta Street
Covent Garden, London
WC2E 8LU England

Typeset in Meridien by Circle Graphics, Columbia, MD

Printer: Sheridan Books, Ann Arbor, MI
Cover Designer: Naylor Design, Washington, DC

The opinions and statements published are the responsibility of the authors, and such opinions and statements do not necessarily represent the policies of the American Psychological Association.

Library of Congress Cataloging-in-Publication Data

Wegenek, Amira Rezec.
  The insider's guide to the psychology major : everything you need to know about the degree and profession / Amira Rezec Wegenek, William Buskist.
      p. cm.
  Includes bibliographical references and index.
  ISBN-13: 978-1-4338-0815-9
  ISBN-10: 1-4338-0815-3
  1. Psychology—Study and teaching (Higher)—United States. 2. Psychologists—Training of—United States. 3. Psychology—Vocational guidance—United States. I. Buskist, William. II. Title.

  BF80.7.U6W44 2010
  150.71'173—dc22
                                                                2009049429
British Library Cataloguing-in-Publication Data
A CIP record is available from the British Library.

Printed in the United States of America
First Edition

Contents

Preface: Why This Book Was Written for You
Amira Rezec Wegenek

I look back in amazement at the fact that I spent over 3 years as an undergraduate psychology major before truly getting a glimpse of what the field of psychology was all about. Sure, I had taken many psychology courses, but as an undergraduate psychology major at a well-respected university, not one of those classes ever provided me with a basic overview of the field. No class covered the career opportunities in psychology or clearly spelled out how much more schooling would be necessary to achieve various careers in psychology. It was not until I became a research assistant at my university that I met a helpful mentor who shared with me the important practical information that was lacking in my traditional coursework. Looking back, I now see how this invaluable advice saved me time and money and helped shape my successful psychology career.

Not all psychology students have the advantage of having good mentors. In fact, only a handful of students are fortunate enough to take advantage of resources that will prepare them for a career in psychology. It was not until I was teaching undergraduate psychology courses at a major university myself that my eyes were opened to the realization that the thousands of psychology majors enrolled in my courses were in the same boat I was in as an undergraduate. At that point, I thought, "If only I could tell them everything I wish somebody had told me when I was starting out as a psychology major." I soon began to incorporate this information into all of my courses and developed a new seminar course to provide an introduction to psychology as a major and career field. I wanted to share all the tips and knowledge that I had learned along the way with any and all interested students. Then, I realized that "all this information would make a very useful book for psychology majors." William Buskist, who is well known for his expertise in the teaching of psychology and student mentorship, came to mind as an ideal potential collaborator on such a project. We discussed this prospect at an annual meeting of the Society for the Teaching of Psychology, of which he was serving as president at the time. With a shared enthusiasm for helping psychology majors, our collaboration began. Thus, this book is the culmination of years of our combined thought, experience, observation, and continual research on opportunities available to psychology majors.

This book aims to serve as your mentor, so to speak, by answering the many questions that you may have about psychology and possible careers in psychology. It provides you with insider knowledge and tips to help you succeed as a psychology major and prepare you for graduate school or a postbaccalaureate career in psychology. It was written to be very user-friendly and offers a unique student-oriented feature called "My Proactive Plan Exercises" at the end of each chapter. We carefully designed these exercises to help you apply what you learn in each chapter to your own career trajectory. We encourage you to keep a notebook in which you record all of the answers to these exercises after reading each chapter. We have also included testimonials from students and professionals, so you can read about real individuals' firsthand accounts of their experiences at various stages of their psychology careers. No matter what stage you are at with respect to majoring in psychology, this book is written for you. Reading this book will empower you to chart your own course in psychology.

The Insider's Guide to the
Psychology
Major

Why Should You Major in Psychology?

1

Psychology is a broad field that encompasses the study of many different types of behavior other than those related to mental health. The psychology major is one of the most popular majors across college campuses and universities in the United States today: Over 90,000 college students graduate with a major in psychology each year (National Center for Education Statistics, 2008a). If you are considering majoring in psychology, you may be wondering, "How do I know if psychology is the major for me?" "Why do others decide to major in psychology?" "What factors influence them to pick this major?" "What does it take to be a successful psychology major?" "What courses will I have to take as a psychology major?" and "What are the 90,000 psychology graduates who received their degrees last year doing?"

This chapter answers these questions and requires you to answer some questions about yourself as well in several self-exploration exercises aimed to help you decide whether psychology is the right major for you. As you learn more about the psychology major, further questions will arise. You should consider this chapter as the starting point in the process of considering whether the psychology major is right for you.

Common Misconceptions of Psychology Majors

Most students who want to major in psychology start out believing that they can become psychologists after earning an undergraduate degree in psychology. This perspective is not surprising, considering that most of the general public has the same common misconception. Contrary to popular belief, it takes an additional 5 to 9 years (on average) of graduate training to become the type of psychologist that most people are familiar with (i.e., a clinical psychologist who helps people with emotional and psychological problems). There are also many other types of psychologists in addition to clinical psychologists. Chapter 3 details types of psychologists, what they do, and the steps required to become a psychologist. Chapter 3 also explains those psychology-related careers that require training beyond the undergraduate degree. Chapter 4 offers information regarding which career options are available to psychology majors.

Another common misconception that many psychology students have is the belief that majoring in psychology is a great way to prepare for a career in which they can help people. Although it is true that some undergraduate coursework can prepare you for a career that involves helping others, most psychology coursework focuses more on psychological theory and understanding the research process. There are also many other disciplines to choose from that specifically prepare students for helping careers, for example, nursing, social work, physical therapy, and so forth. (Refer to Chapters 3 and 4 for further discussion of the many career options available to psychology majors.)

The undergraduate degree in psychology has the potential to help prepare you for a career that involves helping others. The knowledge that you gain as a psychology major also can be applied in many employment settings (see Chapter 4) because the skills that you acquire as a psychology major can generalize to many areas after graduation. However, it may take some work on your part to identify those areas to which your skills might apply. If you are willing to invest the time and effort in finding out about the possibilities afforded to you as a psychology major by doing a little research on your own, it will surely pay off. Reading this book and consulting further references is a great way to start figuring out whether psychology is, indeed, for you.

Why Students Major in Psychology

A recent study comparing self-reported influences on the choice to major in psychology compared data from students majoring in psychology with those majoring in a variety of other disciplines (Marrs, Barb, & Ruggiero, 2007). Psychology majors were most likely to indicate that the number one reason for choosing their major was a positive experience in the introductory psychology course. Compared with students majoring in other disciplines, psychology students seemed to be more driven by interest in the field and the desire to prepare for graduate study. The latter is not very surprising, considering the fact that most careers with the title of "psychologist" require a graduate education. Nonpsychology majors were more likely to report that they chose their major based on more immediate and career-related concerns, such as having a bachelor's degree that would prepare them for a job, a career in a field that would lead to a good salary, and so forth. Students in other majors were also more influenced by the encouragement of a family member in choosing their major. These latter two findings reflect the fact that most people do not see psychology as a traditional major and that the career options for psychology majors are not as well defined as those for some other majors (e.g., business, computer science).

Research also suggests that personality traits may play a significant role in determining which students choose to major in psychology. Marrs et al. (2007) compared psychology majors with nonpsychology majors on five major personality traits and found that psychology majors scored significantly higher than nonmajors on the trait of openness, which refers to personality characteristics such as openness to new experiences, conscientiousness, agreeableness, and extraversion (John & Srivastava, 1999). This personality trait has been related to personality characteristics including intellectual curiosity, imagination, and preference for variety (Costa & McCrae, 1992). Compared with nonpsychology majors, psychology majors also have been found to show higher degrees of empathy toward others (Harton & Lyons, 2003). The findings that psychology majors tend to rate high in the personality traits of openness and empathy are consistent with the notions that many students enter the psychology major out of interest for the diverse subject matter and with the belief that doing so will help them to prepare for a career that involves helping others. (Read the professional boxes in Exhibits 1.1 and 1.2 to find out more about why two professionals chose to major in psychology and their interesting career paths.)

EXHIBIT 1.1

One Professional's Perspective

Michelle Donovan, PhD, People Analytics Team Member at Google Inc.
"Majoring in Psychology Led Me to Industrial–Organizational Psychology"

I majored in psychology in college because I wanted to help people. My dad thought that was great but that I should perhaps be more specific. So, I took out my introduction to psychology textbook and started ruling out specialties. Counseling? Nope; I was a career counselor at our university counseling center and started to feel burnt out by everyone's troubles within months. Clinical psychology? No; I did not want to work with severely mentally ill clients. Developmental psychology? I love kids, but I was not sure I wanted my career to depend on them. And so on. I was simply undecided until I took an undergraduate class in industrial–organizational (I/O) psychology at the University of Wisconsin at River Falls. In that course, I discovered an area of psychology in which I could work with real people in real jobs to try to solve practical, challenging problems.

Finally, I had found my niche. And hey, along the way I would be studying different jobs, so if I/O psychology did not work out, I thought that perhaps I would stumble on another job that fit along the way. With that, another career in I/O psychology was born.

As an undergraduate, two of my psychology professors, Brad Caskey and Rik Seefeldt, advised me to submit three applications each to three types of doctoral programs: my top-rated dream school, a middle tier school, and a "thank goodness I got in somewhere" school. I lucked out and was accepted to one of my dream schools: the I/O psychology doctoral program at the University of Illinois at Urbana–Champaign. I knew I had the grades, a decent GRE score, and a summer research internship, but I was still surprised to be accepted. At the University of Illinois, I worked with my advisor, Professor Fritz Drasgow, on studies ranging from creating and validating tests to designing and analyzing surveys. During the doctoral program, I also completed an internship at a company called Personnel Decisions Research Institutes in Washington, DC. I still remember calling my parents from a pay phone at the DC mall after my internship interviews; I told them I was going to work in our nation's capital to help people. My dad thought that was cool, and my mom wondered where they would be able to park the RV when they visited.

To read more about my career and the various positions I have held along the way, visit http://www.mypsychmentor.com or see chapter 6. Looking back on my career thus far, I think any success I have had is partially due to hard work, supportive managers and colleagues, a strong family network, and plain luck. I always encourage undergraduates in psychology to think about I/O psychology as a career. It is a thriving field (the Society for Industrial/ Organizational Psychology has around 4,000 professional members) and has the potential to have a major impact in how we understand, hire, assign, promote, train, manage, reward, and treat people at work. This is no small feat, as the average American spends about 50% or more of his or her waking hours at work.

Predictors of Success as a Psychology Major

You may be wondering what factors predict student success in the psychology major in terms of academic performance. When Meeker, Fox, and Whitley (1994) measured over 25 possible predictors of overall

EXHIBIT 1.2

One Professional's Perspective

James Wright, PhD, Consumer Psychology Expert and Jury Consultant
"A Hybrid Career in Psychology"

I chose to major in psychology for my pure interest in the subject matter, without any clear career aspirations. Fortunately, it turns out that psychology had the requisite versatility for someone like me, who (at that time) was indifferent to practicality and largely devoid of a career plan. I have since used my educational training in psychology and dovetailed it with practical job experience to generate hybrid business applications of psychology.

My undergraduate studies in psychology introduced me to the applied side of psychology. I used American Psychological Association Internet resources (including http://www.siop.org) to scout graduate programs and postgraduate job opportunities. I chose to apply to industrial–organizational (I/O) psychology graduate programs because it is the subdiscipline of psychology that relates psychology to business (Division 14 of the American Psychological Association).

I enrolled in a graduate program in I/O psychology at Texas A&M University and chose to pursue a dissertation in consumer psychology. Consumer psychology principles are what most marketing and advertising professionals attempt to capitalize on. This educational training, which bridged psychology principles to business applications, was invaluable to me.

When I entered the job world, I applied to a broad range of positions, but my first job offers were in the field of jury consulting (or trial consulting). Jury consultants conduct jury research (e.g., mock trials) to test how a representative sample of mock jurors will evaluate the case facts, evidence, and attorney arguments. This feedback allows attorneys to make adjustments to refine and enhance the way their case is perceived by jurors. Some people wonder how a jury consultant can advise a lawyer when this so-called jury expert never went to law school. It is this training in psychology that qualifies jury consultants in an area of expertise (psychology) that is inextricably a part of our legal system but not taught in law school.

Contrary to popular belief, the high-profile criminal cases are not what fuel the field. Most jury experts are retained in civil litigation matters involving major corporations and claims of monetary damages rather than crimes and jail sentences. My education in consumer psychology translates well to consulting on civil cases because most jurors view decisions about money through the lens of a consumer. Jurors' initial exposure to most litigants is from the perspective of a consumer's frame of reference. Lawyers are essentially marketing and advertising a message to jurors in an attempt to influence decisions—and in civil cases these messages always involve money.

So far over a 13-year career, working for three national consulting firms, I have consulted with corporate entities and law firms in hundreds of legal cases involving Fortune 500 companies, domestic and foreign governments, major network and cable television stations, newspapers and other media, major professional sports teams, athletes, sports franchise owners (including the National Football League, National Basketball Association, and Major League Baseball), boxing champions, Triple Crown horseracing, and major recording artists. The most interesting aspect of the field is the constant exposure to new information; I frequently jump from a case involving computer chip patents to international banana trade litigation to claims of defective children's toys.

I now have my own jury consulting firm (http://www.juryexperts.com). More recently, I have blended my work experience in the legal field with my education in consumer psychology to launch an international Internet marketing firm for the legal industry (http://www.digitallawfirms.com). I also currently author several blogs on branding and consumer behavior. Thus, I am continually finding new ways to apply my educational training in psychology to my career pursuits. (Visit http://www.mypsychmentor.com for a more detailed account of my perspective.)

grade-point average in psychology majors, specific predictors of success emerged. Although interest in psychology subject matter and a positive experience in an introductory psychology class appear to be the greatest determining factors in students' decisions to major in psychology, it is not surprising that grades in introductory psychology courses also have been found to be an important predictor of success. Another predictor of success was grades in general studies courses. Because general studies courses cover a wide range of issues in their aim to provide students with breadth of knowledge, it makes sense that students who might already rate highly in openness do well in such courses. Two more predictors of success were the number of courses taken in mathematics in high school and SAT math scores. This finding might have to do with the fact that psychology majors are taught to understand psychology as a science, which relies on analytical reasoning related to math and the ability to understand statistics. Surprisingly, taking a high school level course in psychology does not seem necessary for students to do well in the college level introductory psychology course or give them any advantage in terms of their performance in the major.

What Courses Are Required?

Psychology is generally defined as the scientific study of behavior and mental processes. It is a broad field with many subdisciplines emphasizing the study of different aspects of behavior (e.g., cognition, learning, perception, development, health-related behaviors, abnormal behavior; see Chapter 3). Most psychology undergraduate programs aim to teach their students to understand psychology as a science, emphasizing psychological theory, the role of behavioral research in psychology, and critical thinking skills. Undergraduate programs do not prepare students to work in a specialty area such as clinical psychology after graduation. Most psychology undergraduate programs these days offer specialized bachelor of arts (BA) or bachelor of science (BS) degrees in addition to the traditional BA and/or BS degree in general psychology. Students usually choose whether to major in general psychology or to major in psychology with an official emphasis in a particular subdiscipline, such as neuroscience or social cognition. Psychology programs define graduation requirements for these specialized undergraduate degrees differently. You may choose to specialize in a particular subdiscipline because of your interests, differences in graduation requirements among specialized majors offered in your program, or better preparation for your future career goals (see Chapter 3 for further discussion).

Table 1.1 offers a partial list of common psychology courses that most psychology undergraduate programs offer. The left-hand column lists the course title, which is either identical or closely related to the name of the subdiscipline covered by the course. The right-hand column provides examples of the types of questions that this course addresses to give you an idea of whether the course content may interest you. Notice that the questions addressed in these courses are all different, but the one thing that they have in common is that they relate to

TABLE 1.1

Common Psychology Courses and Sample Questions They Address

Course title	Questions addressed
Abnormal behavior	How can we better cope with stress to promote wellness and avoid illness? How can we help individuals with psychological disorders?
Biological psychology	What happens to people's brains when they use drugs or sustain a brain injury? Can these changes be reversed? How do biological processes influence our behavior?
Cross-cultural psychology	How large of a role does culture play in determining who we are? How can we use our knowledge of cultural differences to understand one another and promote harmony in our communities?
Cognitive psychology	How do people think? How do people learn? How can we improve thinking, learning, and memory?
Developmental psychology	How do children grow and develop? How can we improve children's lives?
Health psychology	What makes people less likely to partake in risky health behaviors? What motivates patient compliance with medical advice? How can we best promote healthy behaviors? How does stress influence our lives?
Human sexuality	Are men and women really that different? What factors influence romantic relationships? What factors influence sexual orientation?
Learning	How do people learn new information? What is the best approach to teaching a person a new skill?
Sensation and perception	How do we see, hear, taste, touch, and smell? How do these abilities influence us?
Social psychology	Why do people act and feel the way they do? Does the social context of a situation influence personal decisions and behavior? Why do social hierarchies and prejudice exist? How can we eliminate or reduce these issues?

human behavior. You will refer to this table again in completing the self-exploration exercises provided at the end of this chapter. Here are some questions to consider as you look over the courses listed in the table: Does the subject matter of these courses seem interesting to me? and, Might I enjoy learning about these topics? Keep in mind that lower division versions of these courses tend to be survey courses that cover a vast amount of material. Upper division courses allow for more in-depth study of specific subfields in psychology.

Where Are Last Year's 90,000 Psychology Graduates?

According to the latest American Psychological Association (APA) Center for Workforce Studies (2008b) reports, nearly 95% of psychology graduates enter jobs that are not necessarily related to psychology. Over 80,000 graduates enter the workforce each year, and the rest continue on in graduate programs to receive the training necessary to become professional psychologists. About 23% of those graduates entering the workforce enter fields that are closely related to psychology, and 33% enter positions that are somewhat related to psychology (APA Center for Workforce Studies, 2008b). According to the most recent National Science Foundation (2006) reports available, 61% work in business and industry, 30% work in education, and 9% work in governmental agencies. The fact that psychology graduates find themselves entering so many different types of work may be because the skills they developed as psychology majors apply to many work settings. (See Chapter 4 for a discussion of the types of entry-level jobs that recent psychology graduates holding a BA or BS degree typically attain, typical job settings, and job satisfaction among recent psychology graduates.) You may also wish to read books that discuss issues related to the psychology major choice and career prospects, such as Schultheiss's (2008) *Psychology as a Major: Is it Right for Me and What Can I Do With My Degree?*

Are Psychology Graduates Happy With Their Major?

In deciding whether psychology is the major for you, it would be helpful to know whether psychology majors are happy with their choice of major after graduating and entering the "real world." The answer to this question so far seems to be yes and no, based on a large-scale study conducted to address this question (Lunneborg & Wilson, 1985), and depends on whether the graduates went on to attend graduate school or entered the workforce directly. The good news is that, overall, nearly 70% of psychology majors polled said that they would choose their major again. Many students who entered the workforce after graduating from college who did not regret their choice of major expressed regret that they had not combined their major with a career-oriented minor, such as business or computer science. Those students who went on to graduate study found their courses in research methods and statistics to be most useful, whereas those who entered the workforce directly after graduating reported these courses to be the least useful. This finding makes sense because most graduate programs, as you will read in Chapter 5, train their students to be research scientists. Graduates reported that courses in developmental psychology and social psychology were most useful to everyday life, regardless of the career or educational path they chose.

One reason that many students offered for being happy that they majored in psychology was that the major provided them with useful skills. The psychology major fits well with the goals of a broad-based liberal education, providing students with general skills that employers desire. Studies suggest that psychology coursework may provide majors with a better set of skills than other social science majors in the following areas: communication, information gathering, dealing with interpersonal issues, research methods, and ethics (e.g., Kruger & Zechmeister, 2001). This finding suggests that psychology majors receive training that makes them better able to convey information effectively in both written and oral communication, gather and integrate information from appropriate sources, have positive one-on-one personal interactions (e.g., in interviewing, counseling), design and carry out research studies, and take into consideration the impact of projects on individuals involved and society. These skills clearly can be applied to many work settings and are discussed in later chapters of this text.

Is Psychology the Major for You?

One approach to take in answering this question is first to determine your interests and goals and then to judge whether the psychology major and the opportunities that it provides are compatible with them. A useful way for beginning this task is to take a moment to brainstorm and answer the questions presented in the "My Proactive Plan Exercises" section provided at the end of this chapter. The questions presented in these exercises will help you to define your interests and your goals concretely in writing. The exercises require you to think about the answers to many questions involving your personal and career goals, your interest in psychology subject matter, and your personality traits. Answering the questions we have provided will help you determine whether your goals and interests are consistent with the career paths offered by the psychology major. Your answers may also give you some insight into whether you might be successful as a psychology major. Take time to think about your answers and write them down. This step of making your interests and goals concrete by writing them down is essential to the self-exploration process. (You can also read about why one student chose the psychology major in Exhibit 1.3.)

EXHIBIT 1.3

One Student's Perspective

Cristy Sotomayer, psychology major, California State University
"Why I Majored in Psychology"

I had always been curious about the field of psychology but thought that if I got a degree in psychology I would only be able to get a job as a therapist. That option was never particularly appealing to me, so I majored in business administration. A few semesters after I started college, someone suggested that I take Introduction to Psychology because it would help me prepare for a career in business. I enrolled and was shocked to find out that the field of psychology was extremely broad, and there were plenty of other jobs in the field that had absolutely nothing to do with therapy. Shortly after completing the class, I changed my major to psychology.

Although I knew what I wanted to major in, I still was not sure what specific area of psychology I was interested in or what degrees I would need to earn for my career goals, so I did some research. I began asking many of my psychology professors about their specialty areas. Many were happy to help, but most could only offer information about their specific areas. Sometimes the advice that I received from one person conflicted with another person's advice. I was getting confused and wanted to find a reliable source of information all in one place, so I enrolled in a course called "Psychology as a Major and Profession." The course was designed to teach students about different careers and the psychology training and education required for each. In this course, I also learned that having a degree in psychology does not limit you to working in the field of psychology and that skills learned as a psychology major relate to various other professions, including business and sports.

Of all the careers I learned about, a career in research interested me the most. I am fascinated by all that we already know about how the brain works. How is it possible that this matter that is slightly smaller than a football can be so complicated? There is still so much more that can be discovered about the brain, too, and this is what excites me. I know that a career in brain research will not necessarily guarantee that I will make any great scientific discovery. However, with so much more to learn about the brain, I hope that my contributions—no matter how small—will advance brain science and eventually lead some other researcher to someday make that big discovery about the mysterious brain.

MY PROACTIVE PLAN EXERCISES

1. What are my personal strengths? What are my academic strengths?
2. What are my personal weaknesses? What are my academic weaknesses?
3. What are my likes when it comes to reading or learning about new things?
4. Am I willing to learn about prospective careers on my own? If so, what have I done to start this process?
5. Am I willing and able to attend graduate school to achieve my career goals? Why or why not?
6. Am I willing to do volunteer work or work as an intern? Why or why not?
7. What are my primary learning goals in college?
8. What subject matter is most interesting to me?
9. Can I earn good grades in psychology courses? Why or why not?
10. How committed am I to learning? Explain.
11. Am I an inquisitive person who is open to new ideas? Explain.
12. How important is money to me? Explain.
13. Is self-understanding important to me? Explain.
14. Is knowledge of how others feel, think, and learn important to me? Explain.
15. Which three questions about people and behavior presented in Table 1.1 most interest me and why?

Finding Your Path
Tapping Into Valuable Resources

2

I t is normal to be uncertain about your career path and what you will do with your college education. A lot of anxiety surrounds the decision of what to do with your life as well as fear that you may not know all the options available to you or, worse, that you will make the wrong decision. The key to easing this anxiety and feeling comfortable throughout the whole decision-making process is to become as informed as possible. You are already off to a good start by picking up this book. This chapter provides suggestions on proactively seeking information that can help you make informed decisions about your education and career. These tips should help you to narrow down the subdiscipline of psychology in which you might like to specialize as well as help you to develop a list of potential careers that might best suit you.

To Whom Do You Need to Talk?

Talk, talk, talk to as many psychology professors and students as possible! The best way to learn about how to succeed in a field is to ask successful people to share their knowledge and experiences with you. I know, you are thinking, "The professors at my college are so busy, they would probably think that I am a pest if I go to their office hours or e-mail them to set up an appointment to visit with them." Believe it or not, most professors love to talk about what they do! It is not a matter of flattery either. Think about it. What is your passion? Perhaps it is a hobby or sport that you have been involved with for years. Would you not be happy to talk with someone who wanted to learn all about it and showed the same enthusiasm for the activity as you? So, forget about feeling intimidated or as if you are imposing, and ask your professors if you can talk with them outside of class. Do not feel discouraged if you find that the first professor who you approach is not very receptive. Be persistent and try approaching other professors until you find those who are helpful. To read about one very positive experience that a professional psychologist had talking with a professor during her undergraduate years, see Exhibit 2.1.

Of course, there are many other people to whom you can talk who also can share a wealth of different types of information with you. This point is especially important to consider if you do not want to become an academic psychologist and want to instead go into private practice or the business world.

GRADUATE STUDENTS–TEACHING ASSISTANTS

Graduate students–teaching assistants are wonderful people to whom you can talk because, unlike many of your professors, most of them are not too far off from where you are in your career right now. They have recent experience as psychology undergraduates and probably have a clear idea of what career opportunities are currently available. Although most professors may be very knowledgeable researchers and know all about their field, they are not likely to have researched the current job market available to an undergraduate student like you. Graduate students can give you tips on all sorts of things from how to study for your courses right now to how to get into graduate schools and even to which professors might be the most approachable and helpful to you in your department.

UNDERGRADUATE PSYCHOLOGY
PROGRAM COORDINATOR

You may not know who this person is right now if you have never had to seek guidance from your undergraduate psychology administrative office. This person oversees the operation and logistics of your program. He or she works with the administration and faculty to maintain an undergraduate curriculum, handles petitions and special course approvals, and, in

EXHIBIT 2.1

One Professional's Perspective

Tracy Montez, MA, PhD, Industrial Organizational Consultant
"A Career as a Psychometrician in Public and Private Agencies"

When I began college, I was terribly anxious over the notion that I still did not know the answer to the infamous question, "What do I want to be when I grow up?" It seemed that my closest high school friends knew exactly where to go to college and what classes to take for their declared majors that would eventually lead to their chosen career paths.

I, in contrast, went to a local college because it was affordable and declared business administration as my major because marketing sounded interesting. It took only one semester for me to know that business was not my calling. The classes offered to fulfill the business major only partially held my attention. Rather, it was the field of psychology that kept calling me. Despite the intentions of well-meaning family members and friends warning me that listening to people's problems all day would be tedious and stressful, I changed my major to psychology. I knew that the field of psychology must encompass more than clinical work. So, I scheduled an appointment with my undergraduate advisor.

When I met with him, I discussed my interests and my family's concerns. With great patience and understanding, he described the many subdisciplines of psychology. Within an hour, my limited and naive scope of the field of psychology was broadened. In addition, after he elaborated on the discipline of industrial and organizational psychology, I knew that I had found my calling. Here was a discipline that not only "borrowed" concepts, theories, and research from the other disciplines in psychology, but also generated its own theories and scientific findings, applying this extensive knowledge to the world of work.

My initial interest upon entering graduate school was to become a college professor. This decision was primarily based on the enthusiastic and knowledgeable professors that I had both at my undergraduate and master's degree institutions. I soon learned that research was not for me and did not want to pursue a tenure track position that depended upon my publishing research. Although my calling was still industrial and organizational psychology, I needed to identify a specialty in this vast field.

After graduation, I returned to California and began working for a small consulting firm. It is here where I found my specialty, developing selection tests. During my 4-year tenure with this firm, I primarily developed, administered, and scored a variety of tests for all ranks of fire service and law enforcement for agencies located throughout the western United States. As a young woman with an advanced degree, it was challenging explaining to high-ranking male fire service or law enforcement chiefs the importance of following professional guidelines and technical standards when developing and administering promotional tests. They often asked, "How can you develop a test for a fire engineer when you have never driven a rig, pumped water, or fought a fire?" This is where I would elaborate on the value of subject matter experts and how psychometricians used that expertise to develop fair and defensible tests. During this time, I expanded my test development expertise and cultivated my ability to work with different groups of people, which greatly helped me in my next career endeavor, developing regulatory tests for a California state agency and eventually becoming lead psychometrician for this agency. (See http://www.mypsychmentor.com to read more details about my career.)

I worked in state service for approximately 10 years, took some time off to start a family, and subsequently returned to the profession by establishing my own consulting business. I continue to specialize in test development and licensure examination program evaluation.

I am grateful for my education and those involved in the development of my knowledge, experience, and expertise. I could not have completed my educational programs without the dedication of my professors and mentors.

general, advises undergraduate psychology majors. This person will provide wise counsel as to what courses you should be taking given your area of interest, which courses will be available which semesters, and where previous graduates of the department have landed jobs or gotten into graduate school. One of the most important things that you may want to ask this person is which companies former students have gone to work for immediately after graduation. You should also ask about which graduate schools alumni have attended after graduation. Undergraduate coordinators are hired not only for their administrative abilities and communication skills, but also for their desire to help students. Take advantage of the resources this person has to offer you.

PROFESSIONALS IN THE FIELD

Think you might be interested in becoming a clinical psychologist? How about being a management consultant in the business world? Whatever your interests, you should definitely find professionals in that line of work and ask them about their career. Remember, people like to talk about their work. You could contact them and ask them about the things you have always wondered: What was their educational path? Did they need to complete an internship before getting hired? What kind of expectations did they have of their career at various stages? What kind of outlook do they have on the field now, as insiders? What tips do they have for somebody like you, who is just starting out on their career?

You may be wondering where to find these professionals. The first way is to find out whether the career services center at your college (or even a nearby college) has access to the names, phone numbers, and e-mail addresses of alumni who are willing to be contacted. This popular service is one that career services centers have been making available to students more and more these days. If this option is not available for you, then you can locate the names of people in the career that you desire in various association directories, on the Internet, or via word of mouth. Maybe some of your classmates have relatives who have your dream job.

Another good way to find professionals may be to use social networking web sites. Various sites exist that provide opportunities for people to network both socially and professionally. One of these popular sites is Facebook (http://www.facebook.com). Another networking site, which is more specifically geared toward professional networking, is LinkedIn (http://www.linkedin.com). Visit these sites to learn more about how to connect with others who share your interests.

Making the Most of Talking With Others

It helps to have a list of questions you would like to ask others prepared in advance. Having a list will allow you to make the most of your time. You should have a pen and paper to jot down notes, such as names of important books or web sites and so forth. Most importantly, be sure to listen carefully to the advice others have to offer. Of course, you should spend some time sharing a little bit of your history with the person to whom you are talking. However, remember, your goal is to glean information from them. Last, remember never to take one person's response as the final word. As you have learned in your psychology classes, it is best to collect evidence from multiple sources and not to draw conclusions based on a limited sample. One professional to whom you talk may have a completely different take on the future of his or her career versus another based on his or her experiences and personality.

What Free Resources Can Help You?

There are a variety of free career exploration resources available to you. As discussed in the sections that follow, some of these resources can be found on college campuses and others are easily accessible via the Internet.

CAREER SERVICES CENTER

Campus career services centers offer a variety of useful and often free services to students. These services include presentations on different careers, on-campus recruitment with companies, practice job interviewing, résumé workshops, and access to career counselors. Now, not all career counselors are specialists in helping psychology majors find their career path, but they can offer very helpful general information related to the whole process of career development. They are also likely to have had experience with psychology majors who have been successful in their job search in the past and can share what they learned through helping those students. (For information specific to careers in psychology, see Chapter 4.)

VISIT THE AMERICAN PSYCHOLOGICAL ASSOCIATION WEB SITE

The APA acronym is an important one to know if you are thinking about majoring in psychology because it stands for the largest association of psychologists worldwide: the American Psychological Association. The APA is a scientific and professional organization based in Washington, DC that serves many functions: It encourages and promotes research in psychology; maintains codes related to the education and ethics of psychologists; and increases the dissemination of psychological knowledge through meetings, publications, professional contacts, and more. It has 56 separate divisions, each of which represents a different specialty area within psychology. You can learn more about APA and its divisions on APA's web site (http://www.apa.org). Their web site focuses on helping undergraduates; graduate students; professional psychologists, such as teachers and clinicians; and members of the general public to learn more about the field. You will find that the site contains interesting reports on current topics related to psychology that are regularly updated. You should visit this site often and peruse the highlighted news reports and press releases to get a good idea of what topics are important to psychologists today. The site also contains information on psychology honor societies and affiliate organizations and on how to become a student affiliate member of APA.

LEARN ABOUT THE ASSOCIATION FOR PSYCHOLOGICAL SCIENCE

The Association for Psychological Science (APS) is devoted to promoting psychology as a science and its recognition at the national and international level. Its membership of nearly 20,000 includes scientists, researchers, clinicians, administrators, teachers, and students. Its web site, http://www.psychologicalscience.org, contains information about APS and links to many useful resources and current issues. Like APA, undergraduates can become student affiliate members of APS; information on becoming a student affiliate is provided on the APS web site.

PSI CHI AND PSI BETA

The Psi Chi National Honor Society in Psychology (http://www.psichi.org) has chapters at many 4-year colleges and universities. The Psi Beta National Honor Society (http://www.psibeta.org) in Psychology for Community and Junior Colleges is the equivalent society at 2-year colleges. Both are excellent groups to join as membership has many benefits. Students who fulfill membership requirements earn transcript notation of this honor each semester that they remain an active member. Joining such a group is a great way to meet faculty and other undergraduates with similar interests, become involved in community service, and learn about special chapter events, such as guest speakers and field trips. Membership also includes benefits such as qualification for APA student membership status, journal subscription discounts, and more. Read what one student wrote about her experience as a Psi Beta member in Exhibit 2.2 and visit their web sites to learn more.

BROWSE JOURNAL ARTICLES IN THE LIBRARY

Having taken psychology courses, you have already read the summarized results of many research articles. Textbooks generally discuss theory, cover the logic behind those theories, and provide evidence from research findings to support or refute a theory. The evidence is followed by research citations. These citations give credit to the researcher(s) who provided evidence for the claim discussed in the book and lead you to the original journal article that contains a full description of the research methods and the original data.

One way for you to learn what is currently going on within any subfield of psychology is to go the library's periodical section and find scholarly periodicals that specialize in the area(s) of psychology that you find most interesting. Scholarly journals are journals that contain original research articles, unlike popular magazines that merely summarize findings or opinion in the field (e.g., *Psychology Today*). The articles all follow the same format (APA format) so that they can be easily read and followed by psychologists around the world.

EXHIBIT 2.2

One Student's Perspective

Misty Southall, BA, University of California at Irvine
"What Psi Beta Gave to Me"

Psi Beta connected me with a wonderful group of like-minded students. They were very positive and wanted to give back to the community. The friendships that I made in Psi Beta are just one of the important things that I have managed to keep with me from my experience as a club member. Membership in Psi Beta gave me a chance to be involved in chapter functions that helped communities in need that I otherwise would not have had. These experiences have influenced the course of my personal development. For example, I went to a homeless shelter with the club to volunteer one winter evening, where we watched over children while their parents took a "Life Skills" class. This experience humbled me tremendously. I vividly remember all of the children had runny noses. I really felt for them in their hardship and wanted to take them all home with me. Of course, I knew that this would be impossible, but my evening there has stayed with me since. This experience was one of the driving forces that pushed me to seek an internship with Outreach Concern, a school-based outreach program. In this program, I have been able to counsel children on a one-on-one basis at an elementary school in a less than well-to-do neighborhood. Completing this internship will help me to figure out whether I would like to make helping children part of my career for the long term.

Ask your reference librarian to help you find the psychology journals to which your library subscribes. Ask him or her to teach you to use a popular online psychology journal database, such as PsycINFO or PubMed. These digital databases are among the two most popular resources used by psychologists to find literature and can be accessed at most university–college libraries (usually by using a library computer and sometimes remotely if your college library allows students to log in from off campus). Appendix A provides a list of reputable psychology journals to help familiarize you with the range of journals published in psychology. The articles found within scholarly journals are usually peer reviewed, which means that before the article was published, experts in the field reviewed it for quality of research and content reviewed it. APA format requirements dictate that the methods of all research studies be spelled out in precise detail so that other researchers can scrutinize the study and, if they wish, attempt to replicate its results. Researchers rely heavily on journal articles to find out what is currently known about any topic in psychology. In fact, journal articles are much more popular than books because they allow information to be disseminated rapidly and published in a venue that is very specific and for a particular audience. For example, biopsychologists are likely to read *Nature*, whereas social psychologists are more likely to keep up with *The Journal of Social Psychology.*

Once you start reading journals, do not be discouraged if you do not understand some of their content. Remember, these journals are published for specialists and, as such, are going to contain jargon specific to the discipline. At this point in your education, it is not necessary to understand all the finer details, but rather to get the big picture of what the major research questions in the subdisciplines of psychology are and how people go about addressing them. The more you read, the easier it becomes to understand the finer details; do not be afraid to ask your professors about the specifics if you have questions.

Why Should You Attend a Conference?

A psychology conference is a meeting of psychologists that can be regional, national, or international and varies in size depending on the topic and the number of psychologists who are interested in it. We highly recommend that you go to any psychology conference that you can attend. Conferences can be quite exciting, are a great networking opportunity, and will provide you with firsthand opportunities to hear

EXHIBIT 2.3

One Student's Perspective

Christina Mohajerani, BA (Psychology), University of California at Los Angeles (UCLA)
"Why I Am Glad I Attended a Research Conference"

When I was an undergraduate attending community college, I knew that I wanted to transfer to my dream school, UCLA, and major in psychology. I had already taken psychology classes in which I read about research studies that psychologists had conducted. It was not until I attended a regional conference with one of my psychology professors that I really got a first-hand look at what research studies are all about. I attended talks given by some of those very same people who were cited in my textbooks and heard all about cutting-edge research being done in each of their areas. I visited presenters at the poster sessions and asked them questions about their work and about their universities. The conference really opened my eyes to what a vast field psychology is and made psychology come alive for me. It was so exciting to be in the middle of the world of psychology and experience it as a constantly evolving discipline. Attending the conference energized me, exposed me to areas of psychology research that I did not know about before, and gave me a great glimpse into the inner workings of the world in which my future psychology professors at UCLA lived and worked. After attending the conference, I had a better idea of what kinds of psychology might interest me and used that knowledge to find a related part-time job at UCLA that helped me to decide whether psychology was right for me as a career.

the leading researchers in the field talk about their work. You can read about one student's conference experience in detail in Exhibit 2.3.

These conferences tend to center around three types of events: paper, poster, and plenary sessions. Paper sessions about different topics are typically scheduled so that there are back-to-back speakers all presenting research about similar topics. It is exciting to be in a room with people who all share a passion for studying similar phenomena and to hear firsthand about their research findings. Question and answer sessions that take place right after talks can get interesting and sometimes heated. The great thing about attending these talks is that you will often hear different viewpoints about the same topic and be able to see how psychologists from different camps logically argue their points in the name of science.

Poster sessions involve researchers presenting a visual summary of their research in a poster format. The posters are usually displayed dozens at a time in one big room. Poster authors usually stand next to their posters and offer one-on-one explanations of their research. As an attendee, you will get to interact with psychology faculty and students from other schools and get to know them and their work. You will have your questions answered in an informal setting and make interesting professional contacts as well. In fact, many psychologists will carry and distribute their business cards at poster sessions to receive more information from the poster presenter via mail or e-mail.

Most conferences will also offer plenary sessions that are open to all conference attendees. These larger sessions can vary in content and style. Often, they consist of invited talks by prominent figures in the field. A plenary session can also include a panel discussion or symposium, which brings together many experts on a popular or timely topic. Many times, social hours follow plenary sessions and give attendees a chance to socialize and network with plenary speakers and other conference attendees.

You can find a list of major organizations holding annual research conferences and their web sites listed in Appendix B (but be sure to ask around and surf the web for smaller conferences that focus specifically on a topic that interests you, too). You can sometimes even get the registration fees waived if you volunteer to help at the conference. It never hurts to ask the organizers.

MY PROACTIVE PLAN EXERCISES

1. Who are two professors whom I would like to contact to learn more about the subdiscipline or career that interest(s) me?
2. What specific questions will I ask them about the subdiscipline or career that interest(s) me?
3. Who are two graduate students on campus I could contact to learn more about the subdiscipline or career that interest(s) me?
4. What specific questions will I ask them?
5. What is the name of my school's undergraduate psychology program coordinator? What are this person's working hours, and when can I make an appointment with him or her?
6. What specific questions will I ask him or her?
7. Does my campus have a career services center (or similar office) that I can call or visit to obtain contact information for alumni that currently work in fields that interest me? If so, what is the phone number of this center so that I can call and confirm or obtain this information over the phone or via an appointment? If not, what nearby schools might offer such a service?
8. I found the following three components of the American Psychological Association's web site (http://www.apa.org) to be particularly interesting or helpful. (List.)
9. I found the following three components of the Association for Psychological Science web site (http://www.psychologicalscience.org) to be particularly interesting or helpful. (List.)
10. Looking at the list of journals in Appendix A, the following three titles interest me. (List.)
11. Looking at the list of general conferences in Appendix B, there are two conferences in my area this year that might be of interest to me, and here are the dates they are held. (List.)
12. What is my timeline for following up on the important information above?

13. Complete the following action item list:

   Action item   **Expected completion date**
   Contacting professors _____
   Contacting graduate students _____
   Contacting a career services center _____
   Contacting professional alumni _____
   Meeting with my psychology undergraduate coordinator _____
   Further pursuing information related to the APA web site _____
   Further pursuing information related to the APS web site _____
   Visiting the library–librarian _____
   Obtaining and reading articles _____
   Seeking out which conferences I might attend _____
   Inquiring about registration fees for the conference _____

How Do You Become a Psychologist? 3

Picture the following scene. A man lies comfortably on a large leather sofa looking up to the ceiling. He talks while his therapist, who sits nearby in an armchair, asks him questions about his feelings and intently takes notes. This stereotypical image comes to mind when most people think of a psychologist. It is this image of a clinical psychologist that has been made so familiar to us over the years through film and other media. Leather sofa or not, it is true that clinical psychology is a major and important subfield of psychology. However, administering therapy is not the only career option available to psychology majors. In fact, that is why psychotherapists are specifically referred to as "clinical psychologists" instead of simply "psychologists." There are many other types of psychologists, as you will learn in the sections that follow. Contrary to another common misconception, an undergraduate degree in psychology does not make one a psychologist per se. Advanced training beyond the undergraduate level is required to acquire the knowledge and skills necessary to become a bona fide psychologist. In fact, the American Psychological Association (APA) considers the doctoral degree (either doctor of philosophy [PhD] or doctor of psychology [PsyD], described later) the entry-level degree for the practice of psychology.

If you already know that you do not want to pursue a graduate degree, do not feel discouraged about the possibility of finding a job as a college graduate with a degree in psychology. The majority of psychology graduates never become psychologists at all. Instead, they find fulfilling careers that either are related to psychology or rely upon the broad skill set acquired as undergraduate psychology majors. Most psychology major programs equip students with the critical evaluation, problem-solving, interpersonal, and writing skills (among others) that can be applied in a variety of job settings. (Job opportunities for those who hold a bachelor of arts or bachelor of science degree are discussed in detail in Chapter 4). Of the over 90,000 college students who graduate as psychology majors each year in the United States (National Center for Education Statistics, 2008a), only an estimated 16,000 plan to directly enter graduate programs (National Science Foundation, 2006).

Whether you plan to pursue advanced training in psychology beyond the bachelor's degree or not, you should familiarize yourself with the many different subdisciplines of psychology. The APA comprises 56 distinct groups of psychologists called divisions, reflecting the many different types of psychologists that exist and the many career choices potentially available to psychology majors. You should familiarize yourself with this information, as it may prove helpful to you in many ways. An overview of the field will inform your decisions regarding your major, the courses you take, your career goals, and whether to pursue graduate work in psychology.

Many undergraduate programs these days offer specialized bachelor of arts or bachelor of science degrees in addition to the traditional bachelor's degree in general psychology. Students enrolled at such schools can choose whether to major in general psychology (as traditionally done in most undergraduate programs) or to major in psychology with an official emphasis (e.g., neuropsychology, behavioral psychology, health psychology). Psychology programs define graduation requirements for these specialized undergraduate degrees differently. You should seek guidance from your undergraduate program coordinator as soon as possible if you plan to work toward a specialized undergraduate degree. It is not necessary to specialize in a particular subdiscipline, but you may choose to do so because of your interests, because of differences in graduation requirements among specialized majors offered in your program, or to prepare yourself to achieve future career goals. For example, if directly out of college you already know that you want to work in a career related to a specific subdiscipline of psychology, such as developmental psychology, it makes sense to take those courses that best prepare you for that career path.

If graduate training in psychology lies ahead for you, you will eventually be expected to narrow your interests and specialize in a single area of psychology. Taking as many courses as possible in this area during your undergraduate years may help better prepare you for graduate study. However, it is not necessary to obtain a specialized undergraduate degree, nor do graduate programs usually frown upon when applicants hold a degree in general psychology because it ensures that the applicant has a breadth of knowledge in the field. Depending on their respective undergraduate program's degree requirements, it might make more sense for a student to major in general psychology and informally focus his or her studies on one area of psychology by taking elective courses in that area.

In Table 3.1, you will find a sampling of the many types of psychologists that exist, a brief description of each related subdiscipline of psychology, and a few listings of related career fields. Not all of the specialty areas listed are offered as specializations in all undergraduate programs. Notice that almost all of the types of psychologists listed can potentially enter the fields of education and basic research. Psychologists in these fields are considered academic psychologists, whereas psychologists whose primary occupation does not involve basic research and/or teaching are called applied psychologists. Note, however, that clinicians are considered applied psychologists, and some clinicians do conduct research in addition to practicing clinical psychology.

Academic and Applied Psychologists

Just as it requires further training to become a professional, such as a lawyer or medical doctor, it requires a graduate education beyond the bachelor's degree to become a professional psychologist of any type. As a group, professional psychologists can be split into two categories: academic psychologists and applied psychologists. Note, though, that some academic psychologists also do applied work when it is relevant to their specialty area. Roughly half of all psychologists fall into each group (National Science Foundation, 2008b), but this trend may be changing (see Chapter 4). Academic psychologists are often professors, researchers, and educational advisors who create new knowledge, teach, and advise others. Applied psychologists may work in areas such as clinical psychology (e.g., licensed psychotherapists), counseling, school psychology, industrial–organizational psychology, and private industry research. Graduate training in an applied field is usually completed in a different type of graduate program than training for academia, though there are some exceptions. Most applied psychologists enroll in professional schools or professional programs, whereas many academic psychologists earn higher degrees in experimental psychology. Figure 3.1 shows the major divisions of professional psychology, representative subdisciplines or careers, and the type of degree typically required for each.

TABLE 3.1

Psychologists and Major Subdisciplines of Psychology

Psychologist	Related career fields
Clinical psychologists can work in a broad array of therapeutic settings. Most are interested in the application of psychological principles to certain mental disorders, such as depression, schizophrenia, anxiety disorders, and so forth. Some specialize in helping people who have problems adjusting to everyday life situations. Although some are found in academic settings as teachers and researchers, most are found in private practice, mental health centers, and medical centers providing psychological services. Clinical psychologists usually specialize in child, adolescent, or adult clinical psychology. Some work on college or university campuses full time. Clinical psychologists have either a doctor of philosophy in clinical psychology or the doctor of psychology degree. The job market has traditionally been very good for clinical psychologists.	Psychotherapy, community health, research
Cognitive psychologists study human perception, thinking, memory, and perception. Cognitive psychologists are most likely to be found in academic settings as teachers and researchers. More jobs have recently become available for cognitive psychologists than for other kinds of experimental psychologists. Cognitive psychologists frequently collaborate with behavioral neuroscientists to understand the biological bases of perception or cognition. They may also collaborate with computer scientists and scientists from other disciplines.	Research, education, human–computer interface design, engineering
Counseling psychologists are most often trained in departments of counseling psychology. Like clinical psychologists, counseling psychologists may be found in academic settings, private practice, or clinical settings. The job market for counseling psychologists has traditionally been very stable.	Health, education, community outreach
Developmental psychologists study the psychological development of the human being over the lifespan. Developmental psychologists generally specialize in one aspect of development, such as childhood, adolescence, or adulthood. As life expectancy in this country approaches 80 years, developmental psychologists are becoming increasingly interested in aging. Many developmental psychologists may work as consultants to child-care facilities, teen organizations, nursing homes, and geriatric centers.	Research, education, consulting, health
Educational psychologists focus on all aspects of the interaction that takes place among students, teachers, school administrators, and parents. They generally work to develop teacher training programs, selection	Education, research

TABLE 3.1 (*Continued*)

Psychologists and Major Subdisciplines of Psychology

Psychologist	Related career fields
criteria for teachers, and programs to increase student learning and motivation. Educational psychologists focus on instructional design and issues related to curricula and the classroom. They are usually trained in departments of education, where they may receive the master's of education and/or the doctorate of education.	
Human factors psychologists work to design products in a way that takes into account our knowledge of cognition and perception. They apply their knowledge of these areas to optimally design product shape, function, usability, look, and feel. Human factors psychologists work to foresee potential product misuse and to provide consumers with the best possible experiences with human-made products.	Research, education, human factors in industry and government (e.g., Department of Defense)
Evolutionary psychologists study the adaptive nature of behavior. They are interested in how inherited dispositions have evolved and how they aid survival. Evolutionary psychology is a relatively new field and recognizes that genes play a role in determining human behavior. Evolutionary psychologists are usually employed in academic settings and often receive training in experimental psychology or neuroscience with a specialization in evolutionary theory, genetics, and behavior.	Research, education
Experimental psychologists can have many specialty areas. The term "experimental psychologist" is the general name for the combined study of research methods, statistics, and a particular subdiscipline of psychology, such as behavior analysis, cognitive psychology, social psychology, and so forth. Experimental psychologists study both human and nonhuman animals and are trained to apply specific research methods and statistical analyses to their specialty area.	Research, education, consulting, industry, marketing research, pharmaceutical clinical trials
Forensic psychologists apply psychological principles to law and the justice system. Their expertise is often essential in court. They can, for example, testify in court regarding whether a parent should have custody of a child or evaluate a defendant's mental competence to stand trial. Forensic psychologists also conduct research on jury behavior or eyewitness testimony. Some forensic psychologists are trained in both psychology and the law and may be called upon by law agencies to assist in compiling criminal profiles and analyzing a criminal's psychological history when it comes to abnormal behavior.	Law, law enforcement agencies, governmental agencies, consulting, research

(Continued)

TABLE 3.1 (*Continued*)

Psychologists and Major Subdisciplines of Psychology

Psychologist	Related career fields
Health psychologists specialize in how biological, psychological, and social factors affect health and illness. They study how patients handle illness, why some people do not follow medical advice, and the most effective ways to control pain or to change poor health habits. They also develop health care strategies that foster emotional and physical well-being, including those dealing with psychosomatic illness and pain management.	Health, public health, medicine, research, education
Industrial–organizational (I/O) psychologists study the relationship between people and the work place in the interest of improving productivity and the quality of work life. I/O research topics and issues include employee selection, job performance, placement, training, organizational structure, employee motivation, and leadership. They also develop and evaluate tests related to personnel selection and job satisfaction. I/O psychologists can work in business, academic, or government settings, and career opportunities in this field have been ample for the past several years.	Industry, human resources, management consulting, staffing and employee development, research, education
Neuropsychologists (and behavioral neuropsychologists) explore the relationships between brain systems and behavior. For example, behavioral neuropsychologists may study the way the brain creates and stores memories or how various diseases and injuries of the brain affect emotion, perception, and behavior. They design tasks to study normal brain functions with new imaging techniques, such as positron emission tomography, single photon emission computed tomography, and functional magnetic resonance imaging.	Research, education, pharmaceutical research, medical research, rehabilitation
Neuroscientists are concerned with the relationship among genetics, the brain, the nervous system, the endocrine system, and behavior. They often collaborate with scientists in many other biological fields. Some neuroscientists focus particularly on psychopharmacology, a branch of psychology that studies the behavioral effects of drugs in humans and other animals. Neuroscience is one of the hottest areas in psychology and is likely to stay that way for some time. Neuroscientists generally work in research, and there are many job opportunities, though competitive, in a variety of settings (e.g., biotech companies, pharmaceutical companies).	Research, education, pharmaceutical research, medical research
Psychometricians develop and evaluate questionnaires, inventories, and other tests specific to a particular dimension of behavior or thought. They focus on constructing valid and reliable measures of psychological phenomena, such as happiness, self-control, depression and other	Research, education, government, think tanks, political organizations

TABLE 3.1 (*Continued*)

Psychologists and Major Subdisciplines of Psychology

Psychologist	Related career fields
mental disorders, and marital satisfaction. They are usually extremely well trained in statistics and research methodology. Psychometricians are hired to work in a broad array of settings, including political forecasting organizations, governmental agencies, think tanks, mental health settings, and colleges and universities.	
Quantitative and measurement psychologists focus on methods and techniques for designing experiments and analyzing psychological data. Some develop new methods for performing analysis or researching different topics, for example, the efficacy of different social programs or health care treatments. They develop and evaluate mathematical models for psychological tests. They also propose methods for evaluating the quality and fairness of the tests. These psychologists generally have a strong background in both statistics and research.	Research, education, consulting for industry and the government, nonprofit organizations
Rehabilitation psychologists work with stroke and accident victims, people with mental retardation, and those with developmental disabilities caused by such conditions as cerebral palsy, epilepsy, and autism. They help clients adapt to their situation and frequently work with other health care professionals. They deal with issues of personal adjustment, interpersonal relations, the work world, and pain management.	Medical, health, industry, court consulting
School psychologists concentrate mainly on testing (psychometric) and counseling issues in public and private school settings. They consult with parents and school staff and conduct behavioral interventions when appropriate. Most school districts employ full-time school psychologists. School psychologists are usually trained in departments of education, where they may receive the master's of education and/or the doctorate of education.	Education, research
Social psychologists study the interactions among people in groups of all sizes. They are interested in all aspects of interpersonal relationships, including both individual and group influences, and seek ways to improve such interactions. For example, their research helps us to understand how people form attitudes toward others and when attitudes are harmful (as in the case of prejudice) and suggests ways to change them. Social psychologists are most often found in research and academic settings, although they are increasing in number in governmental agencies, business and industry, and private research settings.	Research, education, advertising, industry, government agencies, public health

(*Continued*)

TABLE 3.1 *(Continued)*

Psychologists and Major Subdisciplines of Psychology

Psychologist	Related career fields
Sports psychologists focus on how psychological factors affect athletic performance. They study team cohesion, precompetition anxiety, mental rehearsal, motivation, and personality characteristics common in athletes, among other topics. Sports psychologists help athletes refine their focus on competition goals, become more motivated, and learn how to deal with the anxiety and fear of failure that often accompany competition.	Professional–college–club level athletic teams, research, education

Note. Data are from American Psychological Association (2010) and Buskist and Burke (2007).

FIGURE 3.1

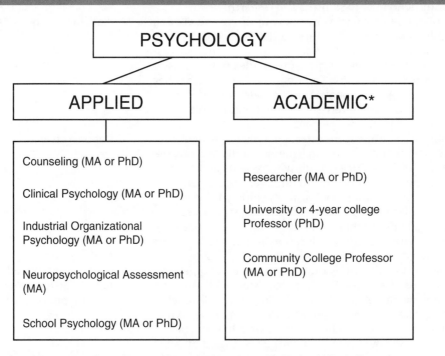

Major divisions of professional psychology, associated subdisciplines or careers, and type of degree required. MA = master of arts; PhD = doctor of philosophy.
*Academic positions emphasize one of the major subdisciplines shown in Table 3.1.

Becoming an Academic Psychologist

Academic psychologists are usually trained as researchers and/or educators and usually work as faculty at universities and colleges. Occasionally, these scientists may work for an institution other than a college, such as a private research institute or a public entity such as the National Institute of Mental Health.

Different colleges and universities differ in the emphasis they place on faculty research and teaching demands. Some college faculty primarily conduct research and publish their original research findings in peer-reviewed journals. Teaching is usually required of these faculty, but most of their time is devoted to building a strong research program. These faculty members may spend much time writing grant proposals to obtain funding for their research, mentoring graduate students, and serving on various scientific and institutional committees.

Not all college faculty devote so much time to research; some spend the majority of their time teaching. However, there are usually fewer demands regarding how many original research publications these faculty are expected to produce each year. At smaller institutions, for example, liberal arts colleges and community colleges, the primary role of the faculty is to teach, not to produce large quantities of research publications and conference presentations.

Regardless of responsibilities of faculty at different colleges and universities, the overwhelming majority of applicants hold a PhD in psychology. To read more about one professional's interesting career as an academic psychologist who conducts applied research, see Exhibit 3.1.

The Doctoral Degree in Experimental Psychology

The PhD in experimental psychology is a degree that involves both coursework and the completion of independent scholarly research. It is awarded in many different areas of psychology, such as behavior analysis, cognitive psychology, developmental psychology, and social psychology. Most universities that offer this degree require students to choose from one of many different specialized program areas when they apply to the program. Many universities and colleges describe their doctoral programs as 4-year programs. However, it is quite rare for such programs to be completed in 4 years. The average number of years for the

EXHIBIT 3.1

One Professional's Perspective

Heike I. M. Mahler, PhD, College Professor at California State University, San Marcos, and Research Faculty at University of California, San Diego
"An Academic Career in Health Psychology"

The patient had coronary bypass surgery barely 2 days ago. He was in the intensive care unit. He had a 10-inch incision down the middle of his chest and another on the lower, inner side of his right leg. There were various wires and tubes leading from his body to a number of machines and receptacles surrounding the bed. Some of the machines were beeping. He was weak, somewhat groggy, in pain, and a bit nauseous. Other patients lay in beds nearby in various stages of consciousness. Nurses, doctors, respiratory therapists, and ward clerks were bustling about. All was as it should be and to be expected, except . . . I was there, with a camera crew. We were setting up lights and cameras and microphones. All morning a little voice in my head had been saying, "You're crazy! You can't film an interview with someone who had heart surgery just the day before yesterday. He's not going to feel like talking, he's not going to want lights and a camera in his face. Even if the patient doesn't back out, there is no room in the intensive care unit for tripods and cameras and lights. Surely the doctors and nurses will have you thrown out when they trip on the cables. . . ."

How had this come about? How did a classically trained social psychologist come to develop videotapes for surgery patients? Let me back up a bit.

I was the first member of my family to attend college. I am the daughter of working-class German immigrants, and college was simply not an option for anyone in my extended family until my generation. I entered college with the goal of a career in criminal justice (perhaps as a police officer or an attorney—I was not sure) and began taking a variety of introductory social science courses (I had been advised by a police chief and other criminal justice experts participating in a career day event at my high school that a social science major such as sociology or psychology would be desirable preparation for a criminal justice career). Although I generally found all of the courses interesting, it was my first psychology class, in particular, that left me wanting more. In short order, I was majoring in psychology, volunteering as a research assistant, and entertaining ideas of going on to graduate school.

After being exposed to research by serving as a research assistant and conducting a study of my own as an undergraduate, I enjoyed the stimulating environment of working in research and decided that graduate school was the next step. I entered the doctoral program in experimental psychology at the University of California, San Diego, in 1981. At the time, all the social psychology faculty members and most of their graduate students were primarily conducting research programs in applied settings (court rooms, police stations, hospitals). My previous training was entirely lab based, and I had never considered conducting applied research. Although the first several projects that I conducted as a doctoral student were lab based, I gradually became interested in applying my previous work on perceived control to surgical patients. I had noticed among my own family members who had undergone major surgery that those who were motivated to maintain control seemed to take a more active role in their recovery and resumed their daily activities more quickly following surgery. This observation led to a dissertation that examined how perceived control over recovery and desire for control over health care predicted the speed of recovery of coronary bypass surgery patients. My dissertation work eventually led to a series of projects funded by the National Institutes of Health that involved the development and evaluation of a variety of videotapes designed to prepare coronary bypass surgery patients and their family members for surgery and recovery. To provide the detailed sensory information that previous literature had established to be important for speeding recovery, and that my colleague Jim Kulik and I believed would instill

EXHIBIT 3.1 (*Continued*)

greater perceived control–self-efficacy, the videos featured interviews with real coronary bypass surgery patients at various stages of recovery from surgery—including in the intensive care unit.

My health psychology research career has been guided by three major goals–principles. First, my work has focused on the dual goals of theory development and application. Thus, I frequently move back and forth between the lab and the field when conducting research. Laboratory work is best suited to the control and isolation of theoretical variables of interest. However, fieldwork is essential for determining the practical significance of variables and for theory refinement. Second, I have always tried to design methodologically rigorous projects. Many of my projects have involved the development of interventions for individuals undergoing major medical procedures. A distorted picture of the benefits of those interventions could have serious adverse consequences. Further, I have made efforts to ensure that my research includes outcomes that the medical community cares about—medical practitioners are not likely to pay attention to health psychology findings unless the relevance to clinical practice is apparent. Thus, rather than exclusively focusing on psychological factors such as anxiety, coping, and social support, my colleagues and I have also collected measures such as speed of hospital release, number of rehospitalizations, and use of medication. Adhering to these principles has resulted in more time-consuming, effortful, and complicated projects than might otherwise have been the case.

My work in health psychology has allowed me to hone the skills I first developed as an undergraduate research assistant. However, it has also provided me with a number of experiences that I never could have imagined as a student. I have written mini-screenplays (videotape scripts); served as a director, producer, and editor; worked with a wide variety of professionals (e.g., nurses, doctors, physician's assistants, producers, directors, graphic artists); and interviewed patients and their family members during extremely stressful and trying times in their lives (sometimes at 3:00 a.m.!). It has required a good deal of work, careful preparation, and, on occasion, turning a deaf ear to the little voices in my head.

completion of a PhD in psychology is 5 to 6 years (APA Education Directorate, 2008). In most programs, the majority of required coursework is completed within the first 2 years. Then, students must take exams or write an area paper demonstrating that they have attained some level of expertise in the field of psychology. These qualifying exams must be completed within a given number of years after entering the program. Usually after this point, students conduct a literature review and spend time working with their major professor to design a series of original research studies to propose as their dissertation study. The student proposes these research plans orally and in writing to a committee of faculty members who are expected to give recommendations, feedback, and approval (if deemed appropriate) of the research proposal. The student is considered a PhD candidate after completing either some or all of these requirements, depending on the specific program, which means that the student has completed all of the requirements for the

PhD degree except for the dissertation. The dissertation can take vary-ing amounts of time to complete depending on the specific type of research involved. Research involving children or animal subjects may pose special challenges that delay its completion. After the dissertation is written, the student must defend it before a faculty committee. The committee members ask the student questions and decide whether the student's work has met the requirements of original and scholarly research required to be awarded the PhD.

Becoming an Applied Psychologist

Applied psychologists can be found working in various settings and constitute roughly half of psychologists in the United States as a whole (National Science Foundation, 2008b). Clinical psychologists work in a variety of settings, such as private practice, hospitals, public and private agencies, and more. School psychologists work in the public and private school systems. Industrial–organizational psychologists work in the business world and with large organizations. Neuropsychologists work in health settings to administer various neuropsychological tests. Coun-selors and social workers are also considered applied psychologists and provide help to people in distress or in need of help that do not neces-sarily require treatment from a clinical psychologist. (See Chapter 4 for career outlooks for several careers in applied psychology.) Next, we dis-cuss various degrees related to careers in applied psychology.

The PhD Versus the PsyD for Clinical Psychologists

If you are considering becoming a licensed clinical psychologist, you may be wondering what educational options are available to you and what career opportunities they afford. Some clinical psychologists hold a PhD in clinical psychology. PhD programs in clinical psychology differ from PhD programs in experimental psychology because the latter provide only research training and do not provide training in the practice of psy-chology. PhD programs in clinical psychology provide a dual emphasis in the development of both research and clinical skills. These programs follow the Boulder model of psychology training, which aims to produce scientist–practitioners who are prepared to work in academia and in practice. PhD programs in clinical psychology are generally housed in universities, though some are also offered in professional schools.

The PsyD is an alternative to the PhD degree in clinical psychology. The PsyD has been officially acknowledged by the APA since 1973 and follows the Vail model of psychological training, which aims to train practitioners in a similar way to dental and medical programs that produce scholars who are practitioners. PsyD programs provide preparation for graduate students who wish to be trained more heavily in practice than in research. However, many PsyD degree programs are now incorporating more rigorous research requirements. PsyD programs have grown in popularity over the years and are offered within university psychology departments, within university-affiliated psychology schools (much the same way as medical schools exist), and within independent professional psychology schools.

Although there was some initial concern that PsyD graduates may experience employment difficulties or stigma in the early days, when this degree was fairly new and not as well known, research shows that there are no discernible differences in employment outcomes between those with PsyD and PhD degrees except that PhD graduates are far more likely to be employed in academic positions (Gaddy, Charlot-Swilley, Nelson, & Reich, 1995). Health care organizations and clients have embraced PsyD practitioners similarly to practitioners holding the PhD. However, some differences do exist between the programs when it comes to acceptance rate and cost. Acceptance rates for PsyD programs are approximately four times higher than for clinical PhD programs, though this rate may vary by location (Norcross & Castle, 2002). Although there may be less competition to gain acceptance to a PsyD program, there are generally more financial costs involved. Tuition assistantships and fee waivers exist to help PsyD students, but their educational costs are not covered as completely as clinical PhD students. It is estimated that 18% of students in PsyD programs receive both a partial tuition waiver plus an assistantship stipend. By contrast, 70% to 80% of clinical PhD students receive full financial assistance (Norcross & Castle, 2002). There is an expectation that PsyD students, much like with medical and dental students, will pay back the educational debt that they incur after graduating and beginning work in their profession. Although PsyD students may incur more debt than PhD students on average, they tend to finish their programs more quickly because of fewer research requirements in their program of study. Students in PsyD programs take, on average, 1 to 1.5 years less to complete their degree than those in clinical PhD programs (Gaddy et al., 1995). See Exhibits 3.2 and 3.3 to learn more about why one student chose to pursue the PsyD over the PhD and about the path of a professional psychologist who earned a PsyD. Regardless of which degree one earns, all individuals working as professional clinical psychologists must

EXHIBIT 3.2

One Student's Perspective

Nicole J. Van Ness, MA, PsyD candidate, Alliant International University
"Why I Chose to Pursue the Doctor of Psychology (PsyD)"

After completing my undergraduate degree, I was admitted to the master's and PsyD programs at Alliant International University (formerly known as California School of Professional Psychology). I recently earned my master's by completing coursework and a practicum, which was done in lieu of writing a master's thesis. The practicum entailed conducting therapy at an approved agency and receiving supervision both on-site and in a practicum class. Five hundred client-contact hours were required. Half of these hours (250) had to be completed doing family–relational therapy. Supervision, training, and travel hours were in addition to the 500 client-contact hours, and a 1:5 ratio had to be met for supervision (1 hr of supervision per 5 client hr). I am currently about to complete my first semester in the PsyD program for marital and family therapists (MFT). My school offers the PsyD degree in both clinical psychology and MFT, as well as a doctor of philosophy (PhD) in clinical psychology. There are a number of reasons why I chose the path of a PsyD degree in MFT.

As an undergraduate, I knew I wanted to go to graduate school, but I knew not how, where, or for what exactly. So, I did some research. Originally interested in forensic psychology, I started there. I wanted to become a profiler for the Federal Bureau of Investigations (FBI). I attained some practical experience by first working in a district attorney's office, interacting with lawyers and investigators. Later on, I got a feel for academic research done in forensic psychology by working on research projects in a laboratory at my undergraduate university. After these experiences and learning that there were only 12 FBI profilers in the Unites States, I decided that I that I wanted something else. My fascination with human interactions and the influence of social context on behavior and attitudes and my desire for more practical, hands-on work experience led me to the field of psychotherapy. I decided to become a marriage and family therapist, with the ultimate goal of becoming a sex therapist.

I knew that more options and opportunities would be available to me if I pursued a doctoral degree and that this degree was necessary to become a licensed, practicing psychologist. My goals were to obtain dual licensure as a marriage and family therapist and as a psychologist. The doctoral degree would not only allow me to practice, but I could eventually supervise, teach, consult, and conduct assessments. I chose to enter a PsyD program instead of a PhD program because PsyD programs focus more on application than on research—though I appreciate research, I did not want to spend my career in research. I was admitted into the PsyD track for MFT at my program. What this meant for me was that I completed the first 2 years of coursework and practicum with the master's students and obtained my master's in MFT. A week after graduation, I continued on and began my current doctoral coursework. It was a great route to take because I can always leave the PsyD program if I decide the master's is enough for me, with little or no consequence. An added advantage of being admitted to the doctoral program and the master's program simultaneously was that I did not have to apply to graduate school a second time when it came time to apply for doctoral programs, nor did I have to do it in the midst of my master's program, practicum, work, or busy personal life.

As I reflect on my past masters work and look forward to my doctoral training, I feel that working with children and families has prepared me for a greater abundance of possible therapeutic situations and outcomes than I could have imagined. With this experience under my belt, I plan to work with couples and families in the future, first as a paid intern and then as a licensed therapist. I will apply for positions in private practice and public agencies, preferably serving the large military population in my community. I plan to focus primarily on couples work as a sex therapist in addition to practicing family therapy.

EXHIBIT 3.3

One Professional's Perspective

Dean Leav, PsyD, Clinical Psychologist, County Metropolitan State Hospital
"My Career After Earning the Doctor of Psychology (PsyD)"

After earning a bachelor's of science in general psychology, I directly entered the PsyD program at Argosy University, a program accredited by the American Psychological Association. My emphasis in the program was clinical psychology. There were various reasons for why I pursued a PsyD degree instead of a doctor of philosophy (PhD) in clinical psychology. I knew after my undergraduate studies and experiences that I was more interested in working with the clinical population than doing research, which is significantly emphasized in PhD programs. A PsyD program allows students who aspire to spend the majority of their time working with clinical populations to focus on that instead of requiring a major focus on research, which appealed to me given my interests. An additional advantage of choosing the PsyD path was that acceptance is generally less competitive for PsyD programs than for PhD programs, which decreased some of the stress of applying to graduate school for me.

One disadvantage of pursuing a PsyD versus a PhD so far is that the PhD is generally more accepted in teaching positions at major universities and in some treatment facilities and the PsyD qualifies one to teach at a smaller range of institutions. Moreover, there are fewer people in the general public who know what a PsyD degree is. One might have to explain what a PsyD degree is to others in such cases until this newer degree becomes as widely known as the PhD in clinical psychology.

My program provided training in such topics as cognitive–behavioral therapy, psychoanalysis, treatment and intervention, and assessment methods and prepared me to be a clinical psychologist. Currently, I am working as a psychologist at Metropolitan State Hospital, an inpatient psychiatric treatment facility that provides service to criminals who generally have the penal code of "not guilty by reason of insanity" or "incompetent to stand trial." I evaluate their cognitive functioning as well as their capacity for reintegration into the community. I also do individual psychotherapy and group therapy.

In the future, I plan to venture off into private practice, where I can work with different populations with less severe diagnostic issues (e.g., higher functioning individuals). I will most likely keep my current job while slowly building up the practice because it does take time.

meet additional professional requirements during and after graduate training (e.g., supervised training hours) before becoming full-fledged, licensed clinical psychologists. (See the Society of Clinical Psychology's web site at http://www.div12.org/ to learn more.)

What Is a Counseling Psychologist?

Counseling psychology programs include PhD programs as well as doctorate in education (EdD) programs and are another option for students who wish to perform work similar to that of clinical psychologists and in similar settings without necessarily working with individuals with severe or persistent mental illness. Historically, counseling psychology as a field once emphasized vocational and career guidance. Today, counseling psychologists facilitate interpersonal functioning and adaptive strategies across the lifespan, with a focus on emotional, social, educational, health, and organizational considerations, in addition to vocational concerns.

Both counseling and clinical psychologists are licensed in all 50 states as licensed psychologists and are able to hold independent mental health care practices. The main difference between a clinical psychologist and a counseling psychologist is that counseling psychologists tend to work with the "normal" client population in need of psychotherapy. Counseling psychologists focus on helping individuals develop strengths and adaptive strategies throughout the lifespan. They may be found working in a variety of settings, including college and university counseling centers, private practices, health care settings, and hospitals. (See the Society of Counseling Psychology's web site at http://www.apa.org/about/division/div17.html for more information about counseling psychology.)

The Doctorate in Education

As mentioned in the previous section, the EdD is an option for some. The EdD is typically awarded by psychology programs that are based within departments of education at a university. Compared with departments that offer the PsyD or PhD, the number of programs offering the EdD is very low. For example, in the 2010 edition of *Graduate Study in Psychology* (APA, 2009), 6 departments out 577 listed reported that they offered the EdD. The primary emphasis of these programs varied, with educational psychology being the most common and counseling psychology also noted as a common emphasis.

Of the APA membership in 2008, those who reported their terminal degree as an EdD were employed in a variety of settings (APA Center for Workforce Studies, 2009). Independent practice was the most common employment setting, reported by 42% of members as their primary work setting; academic settings including 4-year colleges, universities, and medical schools were the primary work setting for 22.2%; and 7.8% were employed in schools and other settings. Provision of mental health services was the most common type of primary work activity reported by 60.7%, followed by education in 14.8% of the sample. If you are interested in learning more about the EdD degree, you may wish to contact the departments that offer this degree to learn more about their programs and the career outcomes of their graduates.

The Master's Degree in Related Fields

Whether you aspire to work in academic or applied psychology, you may not wish to earn, or necessarily need to earn, a doctorate to meet your career goals. Although there are generally more opportunities and higher paying positions available to individuals who hold a doctorate, some professions related to psychology do not require a doctorate degree. For example, one may work as a research assistant, a psychiatric aide at a mental health facility, a personnel manager, or a supervisor in a mental health facility for developmentally disabled individuals with a master of arts (MA) or master of science (MS) in psychology. There would be no call for you to earn a degree higher than the MA or MS if it is not needed for the type of career or work that you have chosen (see Chapter 4). The work of a master's level psychologist can vary from state to state. Therefore, it would be wise to discuss this issue with a knowledgeable faculty member if geographic location is an important factor in job choice. There are also other degrees that may require less time in school than the doctorate degree and do not require training in research methodology that can satisfy your career goals. For students wishing to work in a clinical setting and provide therapy without necessarily earning the PhD or PsyD degree, the marital and family therapy (MFT) degree may be an option. Marriage and family therapists are mental health professionals trained in psychotherapy and family systems and licensed to diagnose and treat mental and emotional disorders within the context of marriage, couples, and family systems. Marriage and family therapists treat a wide range of clinical problems, including depression, marital problems, anxiety, child–parent problems, and individual psychological problems. According to the American Association for Marriage and Family Therapy (AAMFT), marriage and family therapists see clients for mental health problems such as adult schizophrenia, affective (mood) disorders, adult alcoholism and drug abuse, conduct disorders, adolescent drug abuse, anorexia in young adult women, childhood autism, chronic physical illness in adults and children, and marital distress and conflict and tend to provide short-term treatment (12 visits on average). MFT programs are generally 2-year programs, but there are further internship and licensing requirements required to become a certified marriage and family therapist. A good resource to learn more about the MFT degree is the AAMFT's web site (http://www.aamft.org). You can read more about why one student chose this route in Exhibit 3.4. Visit http://www.mypsychmentor.com to find multiple links about the differences between the degrees discussed in this section.

The master of social work (MSW) is a degree that allows recipients to work in similar settings to those in which psychologists work. Most MSW

EXHIBIT 3.4

One Student's Perspective

Kimberly Mounsey, BA (Psychology), California State University at Fullerton;
MA (General Psychology and Clinical Psychology), Pepperdine University
"Why I Chose the Marriage and Family Therapy Path"

I chose to enter the field of marriage and family therapy (MFT) because the rapidly rising divorce rates in this country concerned me greatly. I am a child of a divorced family, and I know how significantly a bitter divorce can impact all members of a family unit. I understand first-hand the far-reaching and damaging consequences these types of divorces can have on each family member's life. So, as an adult, I decided I wanted to enter a profession that worked toward making a positive impact in this area of life. As a marriage and family therapist, people come to you with marriage problems, and sometimes, you are able to work with them to over-come their problems and unite them as a couple once again. However, this outcome is not always the case, and at times the partners may choose to divorce. This outcome, too, can be an opportunity to make a positive impact. With your help and encouragement toward a peaceful dissolution of marriage, you might help this couple prevent making a traumatic event for their children even worse. You have the opportunity to teach them ways to help their children understand what to expect and, most importantly, encourage them to keep the positive avenues of communication open.

Another reason I chose the field of MFT is that you rarely have a boring day! Although some things you hear about in your sessions may be difficult, saddening, or even devastating, I still see each of these sessions as an opportunity to make a positive impact in the lives of my clients. Even when doing something difficult like filing a child abuse report, which marriage and family thera-pists are required to do at times, the end result will be a positive impact on another person's life.

The public is exposed to overwhelming statistics. We hear facts such as half of all marriages end in divorce, which can be discouraging. Of course, I alone cannot have a huge impact on the divorce rate in the population, nor can I "rescue" every child or family as a marriage and family therapist. However, I can help each person that I work with who is in a failing marriage or bad situation to cope with their feelings and to realize that they are not just a statistic, and I can make a positive impact on their lives. Even making a difference in the life of just one client is incredibly rewarding.

programs allow students to choose either a clinical track or a community practice track. The clinical track prepares students to work with clients in various types of clinical practice: psychotherapy, individual or group coun-seling, crisis intervention, case management, child welfare, medical set-tings, employee assistance programs, substance abuse, aging–gerontology, hospice, and more. The community practice track focuses on community organizing, policy analysis, and management in human services. Students who go this route may work for government agencies, nonprofit organi-zations, political agencies, or in similar settings. The clinical track has tended to be more popular in the past, although the community practice track is gaining popularity. The MSW requires 2 years of schooling, in combination with a 2-year internship called field experience. If you would like to research this career option further, a good resource is the National Association of Social Workers web site (http://www.socialworkers.org). Read one professional's account about what it is like to be a social worker in Exhibit 3.5.

EXHIBIT 3.5

One Professional's Perspective

N. Vanessa Vaughn, MSW, Clinical Therapist
"A Career Helping Children"

I first began to consider the field of social work as a freshman at Tuskegee University. Once accepted into the social work program at Tuskegee, I soon learned that there are opportunities in almost every field for a social worker. It was through my volunteer experiences and internship experiences at Tuskegee that I first realized that I wanted to work with individuals within the criminal justice system. I felt an overwhelming urgency to advocate on behalf of individuals who were mostly seen as degenerates who plague society with violence and to decrease the racial and nonracial disparities I saw in the system. As such, I decided that the pursuit of a master's of social work (MSW) degree would be most beneficial to my future aspirations.

After entering the University of Michigan School of Social Work, I was bombarded with various resources and opportunities to gain insight into my prospective field via workshops, alumni presentations, and career fairs. I can recall feeling prepared to work in the field and confident in my abilities as a clinician but unsure about the path I would take to impact the lives of others. For many students, there is a degree of anxiety associated with securing employment following receipt of their graduate degree. My experience was no different. When I reflect on the transitional period between graduation from the University of Michigan School of Social Work and the day I actually began my career as a clinician, I would like to think I submitted hundreds of résumés, as did my cohort of graduates from our esteemed MSW program.

While seeking various work opportunities as a clinician, I worked as a mentor in the foster care system and a direct care worker with homeless youth. I also remained connected to the School of Social Work as a part-time student services representative. As I interviewed for the position of clinical therapist in a community-based treatment program for sexually reactive youth at a nonprofit human service agency, I thought, "This is it!"

As a clinical therapist at the agency, I provide individual, group, and family therapy; clinical testing; individual assessments; and crisis intervention to youth ages 12 to 19 that have been adjudicated of sexual offenses. As a clinical social worker with sexually reactive youth, I focus on issues related to past abuse and/or trauma the youth have experienced and its correlation to their propensity for offending. I also work with victims of abuse and neglect as a means of balancing the emotional impact of my clinical work with sexually reactive youth. Seeking balance in my career, I began to work as a contractual mental health therapist servicing children, youth, and families impacted by abuse and neglect as well. More specifically, I provide intensive home-based short-term counseling to preserve families, reduce the need for out-of-home placement, and prevent the recurrence of abuse and neglect to children.

When working with teenagers, it is my belief that you have to constantly work to ensure they are grasping the concepts and relating them to their lifestyles, past experiences, and/or offenses. In my current positions, I am able to be creative in my approach with clients and utilize nontraditional clinical techniques to foster an understanding of the significance of internalizing and applying treatment concepts. The most rewarding aspect of my job is seeing a family regain trust and hope for a child or teenager they thought was hopeless or a teenager making the decision to take responsibility for his or her behavior and internalizing treatment concepts to prevent further victimization.

It has been a consistent challenge to hear candid accounts of how a child's past experiences can impact his or her life in such a way he or she will never forget. With this point in mind, my career goal is to encourage and support children and youth with turbulent backgrounds in the hope of ensuring that their futures are predicated on their potential and not past experiences. I wholeheartedly believe that if you have the capacity to withstand and overcome the challenges that are presented on a daily a basis in this field, there will always be a career opportunity for you because there is no shortage of children and youth who need someone that will commit to teaching them how to overcome and survive the hardships of life.

MY PROACTIVE PLAN EXERCISES

1. Before I read this chapter, what image would have come to mind when I tried to picture a psychologist? Describe it. Has this image changed since I have read this chapter? If so, how?

2. Would I consider pursuing graduate study in psychology? Why or why not?

3. What type of degrees does the department of psychology at my college or university offer? Does it grant undergraduate degrees other than those in general psychology? If so, what specialty areas are available to students?

4. What are the differences in graduation requirements at my university between the bachelor of arts and bachelor of science degrees in psychology?

5. Which three subdisciplines described in Table 3.1 are most interesting to me and why?

6. If I were to consider becoming a college professor, would I prefer to have mostly research or teaching responsibilities? Why?

7. List the various stages of required work in the doctor of philosophy (PhD) program as described in this chapter.

8. In my own words, explain the difference between a doctor of psychology (PsyD) and PhD.

9. Visit the web site resource listed in the section about the marriage and family therapy degree. Which three pieces of information I learned about this degree were interesting or surprising to me?

10. Visit the web site resource listed in the section about the master's of social work degree. Which three pieces of information I learned about this degree were interesting or surprising to me?

What Jobs Can You Attain With a Bachelor's Degree in Psychology?

4

The psychology major is one of the most popular majors across college campuses and universities in the United States today. Approximately 5% of the 1.3 million freshmen at 4-year institutions select psychology as a probable major (Pryor et al., 2005), and 400,000 students are officially enrolled as psychology majors (National Center for Education Statistics, 2008b). Over 90,000 college students graduate with a major in psychology each year (National Center for Education Statistics, 2008a). However, they do not all become psychologists. As noted in Chapter 3, becoming a professional psychologist requires extensive training and graduate study beyond the baccalaureate. Only an estimated 20% to 22% of recent psychology graduates plan to enter directly into graduate programs annually; it is estimated that only around 5,200 doctorate degrees in psychology are awarded each year (American Psychological Association [APA] Center for Workforce Studies, 2008a). These statistics beg the question, What careers do the over 80,000 psychology graduates who join the workforce each year enter into after graduation?

According to the latest APA Center for Workforce Studies reports based on National Science Foundation (2008a) data, nearly 95% of psychology graduates enter jobs that are not necessarily related to psychology per se. About 23% of these students enter fields that are closely related to psychology, and

FIGURE 4.1

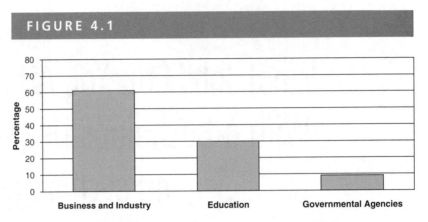

Percentage of recent psychology graduates in different occupational settings. Data from National Science Foundation (2006).

33% enter positions that are somewhat related to psychology (APA Center for Workforce Studies, 2008b). Figure 4.1 shows the three major types of work settings that psychology graduates typically enter. According to the most recent National Science Foundation (2008a) reports available, 61% find work in business and industry, 30% in education, and 9% in governmental agencies. Figure 4.2 shows primary and secondary work activities of recent psychology graduates. An estimated

FIGURE 4.2

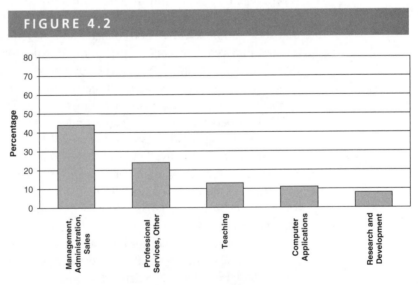

Secondary work activities of recent psychology graduates. Data from American Psychological Association Center for Workforce Studies (2008c).

44% work in sales, management, or administration (APA Center for Workforce Studies, 2008c). Of the remainder, 24% reported working in professional services–other, 13% in teaching, 11% in jobs involving computer applications, and 8% in research and development (APA Center for Workforce Studies, 2008c).

Common Jobs for Individuals Holding Bachelor's Degrees in Psychology

The jobs attained by those college graduates holding a bachelor of arts (BA) or a bachelor of science (BS) in psychology vary greatly in nature of work and job setting. Exhibit 4.1 shows job titles that represent entry-level positions available to recent graduates holding a BA or BS in psychology. Job titles related to psychology, business, and other areas are presented separately. We chose to highlight job titles related to business because the majority of psychology graduates find first-year work in companies as opposed to in other types of organizations. A master list containing over 600 job titles of this type can be found at http://www.dwrajecki.com/job-titles.htm.

How Do You Learn More About Jobs?

If any of the job titles in Exhibit 4.1 interest you, you can use the following free research tools to investigate them further.

OCCUPATIONAL OUTLOOK HANDBOOK

The U.S. Department of Labor Bureau of Labor Statistics offers a free online resource called the Occupational Outlook Handbook (OOH; http://www.bls.gov/OCO), which provides a wealth of information about hundreds of different types of jobs. For each job title, it provides information on the necessary training and education, earnings, expected job prospects, what workers do on the job, and working conditions. The OOH is revised every 2 years to ensure that it is current with newly emerging job titles.

Each job title is presented in its own chapter, or "statement," with each statement containing subsections describing the current and

EXHIBIT 4.1

Sample Job Titles for Those With a Bachelor's Degree in Psychology

Related to psychology

Academic advisor	Gerontology aide
Adolescent care technician	Group home coordinator
Arbitrator	Housing–student life coordinator
Animal trainer	Life skill counselor
Behavior analyst	Mental health technician
Career counselor	Parole officer
Case management aide	Political campaign worker
Caseworker	Probation officer
Childcare worker	Public affairs manager
Child protection worker	Public relations assistant
Clinical interviewer	Publications researcher
Community support worker	Rehabilitation officer
Corrections officer	Research laboratory coordinator
Counselor aide	Residential counselor
Day care center supervisor	Residential youth counselor
Director of volunteer services	Social services assistant
Eligibility worker	Social work assistant
Employment counselor	Urban planning research assistant
Family services worker	Veteran's advisor

Related to business

Administrative assistant	Insurance agent
Advertising agent	Insurance claims–underwriter
Advertising trainee	Intelligence officer
Affirmative action representative	Loan officer
Airline reservations clerk	Lobbying organizer
Bank management	Management trainee
Claims specialist	Marketing researcher
Consultant	Marketing trainee
Consumer affairs	Occupational analyst
Customer relations	Office manager
Customer service representative	Personnel worker–administrator
Educational textbook sales representative	Property management
	Public relations officer
Employee relations assistant	Sales representative
Events coordinator	Small business owner
Financial researcher	Staff training and development
Hotel management	Store manager
Human relations director	Test marketer
Human resources recruiter	

Other areas

Activity director	College admissions officer
Assistant youth coordinator	Community organizer
Camp staff director	Community recreation worker
Church program director	Community relations officer
Church social director	Congressional aide

EXHIBIT 4.1 (*Continued*)

Crime prevention
Director of alumni relations
Director of fundraising
Driving instructor
Educational coordinator
Foster home parent
Film researcher
Hospital patient service
   representative
Laboratory assistant
Neighborhood outreach worker
Newspaper reporter
Nursing home administrator
Park and recreation director

Private tutor
Research assistant
Residential service coordinator
Special events coordinator
Statistical assistant
Statistical reports compiler
Task force coordinator
Teacher
Technical writer
Vocational rehabilitation counselor
Volunteer coordinator
Work activity program director
Youth minister

Note. Data from Landrum and Davis (2003) and Rajecki (2008).

projected future prospects for the occupation. In each occupational statement, you will find a section called "Nature of the Work," which discusses what workers do on the job and the tools or equipment necessary in the occupation. It also provides information about supervision of employees and a discussion of specialty areas within the occupation. For example, the entry for counselors includes a list of specialty counselors, such as substance abuse, educational, vocational, and so forth.

The statement section called "Work Environment" offers information about the typical hours of workers in the occupation, amount of travel, opportunities for part-time work, and risk of injury that workers face in a particular occupation. The "Training, Other Qualifications, and Advancement" section is subdivided into areas that describe necessary education and training, licensure requirements, other qualifications, possible advancement in the field and into other occupations, and estimated employment availability in the near future.

An important section of each occupational summary to consider is the "Job Outlook" section, which provides information about projected employment change and job prospects derived from current national databases. A guide to understanding some of this additional information included in the OOH is also provided online. For example, if a chapter's "Job Outlook" mentions that "opportunities and competition for jobs" are "very good to excellent opportunities," it means that job openings are more numerous than job seekers. If the Job Outlook describes that the "changing employment between 2006 and 2016" is projected to "grow about as fast as average," then employment is expected to increase between 7% to 13%, on par with the average job growth expected in most industries.

The "Earnings" section includes typical earnings and whether workers are compensated by means of annual salaries, commissions, wages, bonuses, and so forth. Earnings vary by experience, responsibility, performance, and geographic area. Benefits such as paid vacation, type of health insurance, and sick leave are not mentioned. Although benefits information is not provided in this general search engine, you should consider finding out more information about what benefits employers offer in specific occupations that you may be seriously considering. Although these benefits are not typically factored into earnings information, they do constitute a major portion of compensation costs to employers and are important factors contributing to workers' job satisfaction.

OCCUPATIONAL INFORMATION NETWORK

You will notice that at the bottom of every job listing in the OOH, corresponding "OOH O*NET Codes" are provided. These numbers are from the Occupational Information Network (O*Net), which is a system that state employment service offices use to classify job applicants and openings and that some libraries and career centers use to file occupational information. O*Net is available to you online at http://www.online. onetcenter.org and is a valuable tool for familiarizing yourself with occupational titles in which you are interested. One helpful feature of O*Net is that it lists job descriptors in different categories and ranks them in terms of their importance to the occupation. The categories include, among other things, interests, work styles (e.g., independence), and work values. The major benefit of exploring job titles using O*Net is that it allows you to search job titles in a variety of ways based on your interests and skills. Exploring O*Net can help you to discover job titles that may increase your awareness of jobs that may suit you particularly well. The "Skills Search" section of the site allows you to select specific skills that you may already have or plan to acquire on the job from a group of six areas, including problem solving, resource management, social skills, and technical skills, before conducting an occupation search.

You can search for occupations in the "Find Occupations" section of O*Net in a variety of ways in addition to searching by related skills. First, you can search by keyword by entering a word, phrase, partial or full occupation code, or job title. Next, you also can explore occupational titles by viewing those identified as "High Growth Industries" that are projected to add substantial numbers of new jobs and are being transformed by new innovations, including new technologies. An area of the site called "Job Zone" groups occupations on the basis of level of education, training, and experience or training necessary to perform the occupation. You can also search the "Job Families" area to find groups of occupations organized by type of work performed, skills, education, training, and/or credentials needed. You also can search the "STEM" discipline section to find occupations specifically related to science, technology, engineering, and mathematics. It is worthwhile to try different approaches to searching job titles within O*Net, as you may discover possibilities that you may not have considered before.

Will You Be Qualified for the Job With a BA or BS in Psychology?

The jobs listed in Exhibit 4.1 are quite varied. The one thing that they have in common is that they are all typically considered entry-level positions by most resources providing information regarding jobs available to people with an undergraduate degree in psychology. However, you may notice when researching the job titles that they vary greatly in terms of the type of experience required. In fact, a recent study has shown that so-called entry-level positions may even differ in terms of how much education is required to attain them. Rajecki (2008) investigated the education required to attain many of the entry-level positions that are usually included in most print and online occupational resources for psychology graduates. He found that some titles (e.g., child care worker, residential advisor, statistical assistant) may not require a bachelor's degree. Other titles listed, such as human resources manager or rehabilitation officer, required either education or experience beyond the baccalaureate, according to information from the U.S. Bureau of Labor and Statistics.

The information from OOH and O*Net suggests that some psychology graduates may take any job that they can get when initially entering the workforce and may purposefully take positions for which they are overqualified to achieve a stepping stone to a higher level position. For example, a recent psychology graduate may take an advertising sales agent position as a stepping stone to a future higher level position in advertising. This approach would be a beneficial one, especially for someone with little or no work experience. It is also promising to note that studies suggest that having a college education puts applicants at an advantage because employers often seek employees with at least some college experience and are often willing to provide extensive on the job training to them (U.S. Bureau of Labor and Statistics, 2006).

The OOH and O*Net data also suggest that some individuals who hold a bachelor's degree in psychology will be underqualified for positions coming out of college if they do not have prior work or internship experience within an organization or company. For example, positions such as sales manager, public relations manager, and human resources manager require significant on-the-job experience to attain (Rajecki, 2008). (See Chapter 5 for a discussion of how to find volunteer and internship positions that can provide you with résumé-enhancing skills and experience.) Some occupational listings actually require a master's degree (e.g., urban and regional planner, substance–behavioral disorders counselor, marriage and family therapist, rehabilitation counselor). Refer to Exhibit 4.2 to read about one professional who holds a B.A. in psychology and her experience working for a state agency.

Last, many of the lists of entry-level jobs geared toward psychology graduates provided in online and print resources give the false impression that the jobs listed can be attained with only a bachelor's degree in psychology. However, many job titles included on such lists actually require further training or experience beyond the baccalaureate. This situation may be due to the fact that such lists err on the liberal side of being widely inclusive, which is understandable because such lists are meant to appeal to a broad range of students and their wide array of interests and aptitudes. Knowing about the liberally inclusive nature of such lists should provide you with one more reason to be proactive and research job titles that you may be interested in on your own. This approach is the only sure-fire way to gauge whether the job prospects that you may be entertaining are a good match for your interests, skills, and career goals. If you are interested in learning more information

EXHIBIT 4.2

One Professional's Perspective

Jessica Booth, MA
"Skills I Learned as a Psychology Major"

I earned my bachelor of arts in psychology from California State University, Fullerton, in May 2008. I currently work for a local city in urban planning and am responsible for approving residential, commercial, and industrial development within the city. Although I worked part-time for the city prior to graduating, allowing me 2 years of job training, obtaining my psychology degree allowed me to become a full-time employee after graduation. In general, many jobs, especially government jobs, prefer an applicant to have a degree in a certain field but will also consider applicants with degrees in similar fields. Psychology is one field of study that many employers find advantageous because graduates have obtained important skills in interpersonal communication, research and data collection, and human behavior recognition.

I believe that the most important skills I learned from studying psychology were research and data collection as well as subsequent report writing skills. Working in urban planning, I am frequently researching the history of certain properties trying to find specific details about them. Knowing how to conduct research and locate documents is definitely an asset that I use on a daily basis. Additionally, having the skills to compile information into a concise, detailed report is valuable as well. Overall, I believe that earning a psychology degree has allowed me the opportunity to explore many different occupations that might not have been open to me with a degree in another field.

relevant to careers available to psychology graduates, read the excellent resource books by Landrum (2009) and Sternberg (2007).

Are Recent Psychology Graduates Satisfied With Their Jobs?

Many students become psychology majors with unrealistic expectations of what careers their coursework will prepare them to enter. As discussed in Chapter 1, many students enter the major because they are interested in helping others or because of a positive experience in their introductory psychology course. Many students even think that a bachelor's degree in psychology will enable them to become psychologists, a common myth that is noted in Chapter 3. Most beginning psychology majors do not realize that the majority of psychology coursework does not provide students with any training directly relevant to helping others and is not vocationally oriented. Psychology undergraduate programs do, however, equip students with many valuable skills, such as communication and critical thinking skills, that can be applied to a very wide range of possible work settings. This fact, combined with students' misperceptions about the type of preparation afforded by their undergraduate coursework in psychology, helps to explain why many recent psychology graduates in their first year of employment after graduation find themselves less than satisfied in their positions. In turn, this point may lead many recent psychology graduates to find themselves working in fields that they had not originally planned to enter. Adding to the lack of satisfaction seen in first-year employment for psychology graduates may be that employment satisfaction appears to be tied to how well one's major is directly related to the nature of employment for most students (e.g., Kressel, 1990), and nearly 95% of psychology graduates enter careers that are not specifically related to psychology. (You can read about one professional's career helping others that did not require a graduate degree in Exhibit 4.3.)

How Realistic Are Your Expectations?

As a psychology major, you can expect to acquire many useful skills that employers in many fields value. Thus, majoring in psychology opens up a broad range of possible work settings. However, this variety must be

EXHIBIT 4.3

One Professional's Perspective

Tom Offerdahl, Certified Substance Abuse Counselor,
Owner of Embrace Recovery, Addiction Treatment Center
"A Career Helping Others"

Growing up in Hawaiian Gardens, California, I remember I always wanted to be a teacher. Unfortunately, I was one of seven kids, and college was not something we could afford. So instead I got a job at the phone company as a telephone operator and worked my way up to service representative. I developed carpal tunnel syndrome, however, and was forced to look into a new career. I went to a local community college and took a vocational test to help me determine a career path. . . . It said I should become a mortician! No thanks.

I was 5 years clean and sober at that time, and my roommate was a drug and alcohol counselor. So I interviewed several people who we were drug and alcohol counselors to determine whether I would have to do any repetitive handwork, as I was limited with carpal tunnel syndrome. It turned out that physically, I was fit for that type of job. More importantly, I would finally be able to realize my dream of being a teacher—teaching people who suffer from addiction how to get sober and reclaim their lives. I myself never had any treatment for addiction; I got sober through Narcotics Anonymous and with the help of a wonderful licensed clinical social worker.

Saddleback College offered a certification program for alcohol and drug counselors, in which I enrolled in 1995. One of my internships was at South Coast Medical Center. It exposed me to detoxification and inpatient and outpatient treatment for alcoholism and addiction.

My first job in the field of recovery was at a residential treatment program in 1996. I facilitated both process and education groups, as well as their PC1000 program. PC1000 is a court-ordered program for first-time offenders guilty of driving under the influence. I fell in love with my career choice. Being a drug and alcohol counselor is the most rewarding thing I have ever done, and I received positive feedback from my peers and clients, so I knew I was on the right path.

After 1 year, I was able to get a job on the Genesis Unit at South Coast Medical Center. Originally, their chemical dependency unit was combined on the second floor with their behavioral health unit. So, in addition to being a drug and alcohol counselor, I was also introduced to working with people with comorbid disorders, such as depression and addiction. I was also put in charge of running the weekly family group, which allowed me to learn and to help family members dealing with loved ones who suffer from addiction. Many of these family members attended weekly meetings for up to 5 years, and it has helped me see how recovery takes place in, and impacts, the whole family unit.

When the Genesis Unit was taken over by a new program, I was once more challenged. The new program was larger in scale with more components and was not a nonprofit program, as the Genesis unit was. It became clear over time that their vision of how to treat addiction was different from my own. As a result, I opened up my own outpatient program for addiction. I cofounded it with my mentor, who has worked in the field for 18 years and is the best drug and alcohol counselor that I know.

Running my own treatment center for addiction is the scariest and most exciting thing I have ever done. I am no longer encumbered by administration and can finally treat people as individuals with individual needs. More importantly, I am able to set a limit for how many clients we take on at a time. We decided on eight clients, as our years of experience show that any more than that and the clients would not benefit because they literally get lost in the crowd. Our evening outpatient program has been so successful that we are adding a day outpatient program as well. Embrace Recovery (the name of our program) is celebrating its 1st anniversary.

I love my work and continue to grow and learn as a counselor. I am passionate about what I do and feel it is so important to maintain the integrity of the field of addiction. We offer an internship program where counselors can get hands-on experience as drug and alcohol counselors. It also helps me to guide those individuals who, though they may be well meaning, do not possess the skills to be effective counselors.

reconciled with the finding that many psychology graduates in their first year of employment after graduation are not satisfied with their jobs (Rajecki, 2008). However, first-year employment data reflecting low levels of job satisfaction among recent graduates may not be indicative of future job satisfaction because they only reflect satisfaction in entry-level positions. It is not surprising that entry-level positions are not as satisfying because they usually do not directly relate to major or offer high pay. We can assume that the recent graduates surveyed will not remain in entry-level positions for the long term; although first-year employment may be less than satisfactory, the long-term outlook for psychology graduates may be more positive.

Relative to individuals who did not graduate from college, psychology (and other liberal arts) alumni can expect more upward mobility (Stringer, 2000–2001). Even in those occupations that do not require a college degree, psychology (and other college) graduates tend to earn more than those persons without a college degree because they are more likely to receive further training and promotions (Crosby, 2000–2001).

Which Job(s) Might You Find Satisfying?

Figuring out what you want to do with your life is neither a simple nor an easy task. In fact, it is estimated that most of us are continually working to figure this point out, with an estimated 10 job changes expected for the average American between the ages of 18 and 38 (U.S. Bureau of Labor Statistics, 2000). There are many factors that you should consider in choosing a career. For example, you will want to consider the current economic opportunity outlook for different positions, whether the work environment and required skills are a good match for you, and the growth potential when comparing occupational titles that appeal to you. You should also consider how much more training or education you are willing to seek to attain the career of your choice.

One thing to keep in mind when weighing all these factors is that income has not been found to be the greatest determinant of job satisfaction. Multiple studies have suggested that one of the greatest determining factors of job satisfaction among workers is the perception that their jobs match their higher goal commitments in life and help them to attain these goals (e.g., Roberson, 1990). Therefore, the process of career exploration inevitably involves a high degree of self-exploration. Read Exhibit 4.4 to learn about one student's experience in this self-exploration process that eventually led to her landing her first full-time job. The exercises provided at the end of this chapter will help you in this process.

EXHIBIT 4.4

One Student's Perspective

April Le, BA (Psychology), University of California, San Diego
"How I Found My First Job"

In my senior year of college, it was discouraging to admit to my parents (and to myself) that I still was not exactly sure what I wanted to do after graduation. To make matters worse, it felt as though many of my peers in more traditional majors already had their career plans mapped out. After a while, I came to realize it was okay that I did not know—as long as I continued to work hard in the classroom and committed myself to following a strategic career exploration plan on my own time.

As a psychology student, you find that research makes up a large part of the academic curriculum, and you are taught about various methodologies involved in conducting research. Unfortunately, we neglect to apply these methods in how we conduct our own lives when it comes to researching and identifying a fitting career. In my opinion, the challenge in finding your career does not necessarily lie in figuring out what you want to do. It lies in gathering all the information necessary to enable you to make the best possible career decision.

I approached my job search like a research study, recruiting participants to interview, composing relevant interview questions, identifying correlations in the accumulated data, and keeping up with job market news and literature. It was through this process, combined with a "go-getting" attitude, that I landed my first postcollege job. It was clear I needed exposure to various people in different industries to understand where my individual strengths and interests could develop, and I went outside of my school environment to find such people and work environments. One of the ways I did so was by joining a biotech networking forum (because there was not one for psychology at the time), with hopes that I could establish informational meetings and learn from people with varying backgrounds and experience.

I met various people at this forum and, at one of the meetings, a woman from a local pharmaceutical company came to talk about her work in conducting clinical trials. Her work involved analyzing data from thousands of health records and using it to research and make drugs that would improve people's health. After her talk, I mentioned to her that her work sounded really interesting and that I wanted to know where I could get exposure to the industry. She was happy to help when she learned that I was exploring careers that utilized classroom psychology principles. To obtain a "bird's eye" view of the industry, she suggested I take an internship within her company's global clinical trials department. The internship entailed processing data from clinical trial patients all over the world. Though this job was not glamorous by any means, it provided me with a unique experience to learn about health care (or lack of it) in the world's developing countries. Moreover, I had the opportunity to understand and apply a multitude of subjects from classroom learning on the job. To think I almost chickened out and went home instead of staying after her talk!

During my internship, I continued to seek informational interviews and set up arrangements with professors and professionals at several companies to learn about other career paths. This focus helped me create short-term shadowing, apprenticeship, and educational opportunities. During spring break, I researched 20 companies in my city's industrial district and went door-to-door with my résumé. I was ecstatic to find somebody at most of these companies who sat down with me and described the various job roles within their companies. I met people with various backgrounds, skill levels, job titles, and degrees. One thing that never changed was the willingness that these people demonstrated to help a curious undergraduate as she conducted her own career research project.

After more than a year of such activities, I gained enough knowledge, exposure, and job skills to know what I wanted to do within the field of pharmaceutical clinical trials research and land a full-time job doing just that after graduation.

MY PROACTIVE PLAN EXERCISES

1. Choose one occupational title from Exhibit 4.1 that interests me. Look it up at the Occupational Outlook Handbook (OOH) web site. Describe the specific information that I learned about the job. Explain which section of the job summary I found most helpful or important to me.

2. Now search the same job title that I chose in the first exercise using the Occupational Information Network (O*Net) web site. What additional information did I learn about the job? What additional information did O*Net offer that I did not find in my search using OOH?

3. Perform a search for job titles in O*Net based on different skills. Choose which skills I have to offer or hope to develop on the job from the list in Exhibit 4.1. Write down those skills for my records.

4. Which job titles did my O*Net search based on skills return? List the job titles. Had I considered these job titles before?

5. Think about what is important to me in my life now and decide on some of the larger goals that I would like to achieve in my life. What potential job listings from Exhibit 4.1 do I think may be in line with those larger goals?

6. Search two of the potential job listings that I think may help me to attain my life goals using OOH and O*Net. Was what I found in my search consistent with my initial expectation of what the job duties, work environment, skills, and so on would be like?

Graduate School 5

f you have decided on a career path that requires education beyond the associate's or bachelor's degree, you will need to apply to graduate school programs. This chapter addresses questions and issues relevant to the graduate school program application and selection process and offers advice for anyone considering application to experimental psychology or clinical psychology master's and/or doctoral programs. As mentioned in Chapter 3, experimental psychology programs differ from other programs in that they provide primarily research training, whereas clinical psychology doctoral programs provide training in both research and therapy to prepare students as researchers and clinicians. This chapter offers critical information you can use that may give you an edge when it comes to choosing, applying to, and getting accepted into the right experimental psychology graduate program that suits you and your professional goals. The doctor of psychology (PsyD), master of social work (MSW), and marriage and family therapy (MFT) degree programs (see Chapter 3) do not emphasize research training but do value both research and practicum training in applicants (see Chapter 3 for a more detailed discussion of the differences between these programs).

Graduate Schools and Graduate Programs

A graduate school is an administrative body, usually directed by a dean, and creates policies regarding all graduate programs within a college or university. A graduate program is a group of faculty members organized around a particular subfield or subdiscipline, such as a graduate program in cognitive psychology or clinical psychology. These programs create their own admissions processes and criteria. At colleges and universities that have a centralized graduate school, the application for a particular program is submitted to the graduate school. At schools that do not have centralized graduate schools, the application is submitted to the department in which the program resides (e.g., psychology or cognitive science) and then is forwarded to a selection committee within the graduate program. If you are applying for a doctor of philosophy (PhD) in psychology, you should decide on which program area(s) you want to specialize in before applying for admission.

Students often think that if they apply to a graduate school program that is ranked higher in national graduate school rankings than another graduate school overall, it is necessarily a better program. For example, the National Research Council and *U.S. News and World Report* both provide annual national rankings for graduate programs in psychology based on overall statistics, such as amount of grant money obtained and number of publications written by faculty. However, it is not true that a graduate school's national rankings necessarily reflect the esteem of each of its individual programs. For example, a very prestigious Ivy League school may have an excellent social psychology program with several faculty members who are famous in that field, but it may not have a very well-developed biological psychology or cognitive psychology program. Different graduate schools offer different strengths and weaknesses within each of their program's areas that are not always evident in overall graduate school rankings. However, individual program reputations can be discovered through a little research, as we describe later in this chapter.

The Graduate School Program Admissions Process

The typical graduate school program admissions process requires several components and involves multiple stages. Undergraduate applicants should e-mail departments requesting admissions materials no later than

September of their senior year. Waiting longer may make it impossible for you to meet some of the earlier deadline requirements (e.g., January 1). The application is usually not considered complete until the graduate school receives the following items:

- application form,
- letter of intent,
- transcripts,
- letters of recommendation,
- GRE scores,
- other materials required by the program, and
- an application fee.

Graduate schools forward completed applications to the appropriate admissions committee, which is usually made up of departmental administrators, faculty, and, sometimes, graduate student representatives. Admissions committees or the graduate program coordinator usually prescreen applications and then select some applicants to be interviewed by faculty. Some programs conduct interviews over the phone, whereas others conduct them in person. Students usually incur some travel costs to attend on-campus interviews, though some programs may subsidize these costs.

How Difficult Is It to Get Into Graduate School?

Acceptance to graduate programs is extremely competitive, especially for highly regarded PhD programs. Clinical programs often have the most competitive entrance requirements. These very competitive programs typically admit students with a grade-point average (GPA) of 3.8 to 4.0, and the typical GRE score may be in the 1300 plus range. Other programs are less competitive, although the typical GPA of their students is still fairly high—generally in the 3.3 to 3.5 range.

If your GPA is in the lower range, you may wish to consider applying to master's programs if you do not get admitted into a PhD program. Performing at the "A" level in these programs can put you in a better position to be accepted into a PhD program in the future. Some undergraduate programs offer a master's program called a "5th-year program." The 5th-year program allows you to earn both your bachelor's and master's degree by adding 1 more year to the time it would normally take you to complete the bachelor's degree. During this year, you would take graduate-level courses and possibly complete a research project. Some 5th-year programs are accelerated graduate programs in which you earn your master's degree in 1 year. Whether you choose a 5th-year or traditional 2-year master's degree program, be aware that most PhD programs will require you to have completed a thesis in your master's program. The thesis is a written report of independent research. If you complete a master's program that does require a thesis and later apply to a graduate PhD program, the program may require you to complete a thesis after admission. There is another caution to consider if you plan to apply to a PhD or PsyD program after completing a master's program: Some doctorate programs do not accept transfer credits or master's thesis work completed in other programs and may require students to start over, increasing the time spent in school and cost.

If your GPA is low and you still wish to consider applying to PhD programs, there are some factors that might compensate for your low GPA. If you have a modest GPA (e.g., 3.2) but high GRE scores (1200 plus), a strong letter of intent, strong clinical or research experience, and great letters of recommendation, you may still be a viable applicant to competitive programs. However, high GRE scores do not necessarily make up for weak letters of recommendation or a weak letter of intent.

What Admissions Committees Look for in Applicants

Admissions committees are looking for applicants who are well prepared to begin graduate-level studies, are a good match to work with at least one faculty member in their program, have a good likelihood of success in the program, and know what they are getting themselves into. You can work to attain all of these attributes in almost any undergraduate program, big or small. You should try to perform your best academically to become well prepared for graduate-level studies and earn a high GPA. You should research programs carefully to gauge whether a program and its faculty members might be a good fit for you. Doing well academically, scoring high on standardized tests such as the GRE, and obtaining great letters of recommendation will serve as indicators of your potential for success in a graduate program.

One important step that you can take to become a stronger candidate (and that will help you to get a better idea of what is likely in store for you as a future graduate student) is to become involved in research during your undergraduate years. In fact, a survey in the 1990s asked clinical psychology admissions committees what the most important factors besides GPA and GRE scores were in developing the appropriate credentials for becoming a graduate student. Admissions committees listed research experience and letters of recommendation as the most heavily weighted factors (Stroup & Benjamin, 1982). These results likely reflect the feelings of many or most faculty that serve on admissions committees, not just clinical faculty.

Getting Involved in Research

Whether your own personal goal is to become a research psychologist, clinical psychologist, or educator or to go into industry, one of the most important things that you can do as an undergraduate psychology major is become involved with a research project. Do not be shy about contacting your professors or their graduate students in person or via e-mail to inquire about becoming involved in their research. You should ask them whether they have any volunteer, paid, or course-credit-earning positions open in their laboratory. If so, you should meet with them to discuss what type of project you can get involved with and what your duties would include to decide whether a particular laboratory position seems right for you. It may be more difficult to get research experience at some institutions than others. For this reason, do not feel as if the project that you work on has to be one that you are particularly interested in or the ideal project because your objective is to gain research experience in general. Any research experience is better than no research experience, and it will allow you to discover elements of the research process that you do and do not enjoy as well as to understand better what type of research you would or would not like to pursue in the future.

Research involvement allows you to get a firsthand look at what the research process is like, learn analytical and computer skills, and work with others. All these are practical skills that are applicable in the "real world" and academia. Becoming involved in research also allows you to get to know faculty members on a personal level. Most laboratories have regular meetings or regular journal discussion group meetings. Laboratory meetings usually involve all laboratory members, including the principle investigator (PI; usually the faculty who heads the laboratory), gathering to discuss ongoing projects. Journal club meetings usually involve a group meeting to discuss selected journal articles that are related to the group's research interests. In either type of meeting, it is common for a member to present research or lead a discussion on a research-related topic and for the faculty to interact with attendees. If you join a laboratory, you may end up working closely with a faculty member's graduate student or postdoctoral researcher. Although you will receive experience in research working mostly with this person, the laboratory and journal club meetings are great opportunities to interact with the PI directly. You may also wish to schedule personal appointments

EXHIBIT 5.1

One Student's Perspective

Michelle Robison, BA, MA (Experimental Psychology), California State University Fullerton
"How Volunteering in Research Helped Me"

Getting involved as an undergraduate research assistant in different psychology laboratories was advantageous for me in a number of ways. First, I got to dabble in all aspects of the research process. I got the experience of doing a literature review, contributing ideas for methodology, collecting data, analyzing data, and writing parts of a paper. These research skills are essential to have, especially for somebody like me, who was considering entering graduate school. Second, I had an opportunity to establish relationships with professors I worked with and other students in the laboratory. These relationships have created opportunities and networking tools helpful for gaining graduate school admission and jobs. Third, being a research assistant allowed me to explore different areas of psychology to figure out where my interests fit best, which increased my knowledge of the field of psychology and helped me realize that I wanted to continue doing research in the field in which I had initially started. Finally, being a research assistant created a sense of responsibility and empowerment in me. It gave me the ability to contribute collaboratively and independently to important research projects and to prove my commitment to the field of psychology to myself and others.

with the PI or attend appointments with your mentor (graduate student or postdoctoral supervisor) and the PI that are related to the project to which are assigned. Knowing the PI will give you more personal exposure to what it is like to be a faculty member at your college and will likely result in the PI writing you a more powerful and personal letter of recommendation (see the "Who to Ask for Letters of Recommendation" section). You can read about how volunteering in a laboratory was beneficial to one student in Exhibit 5.1.

What if You Attend a Small Undergraduate Institution?

If you come from a small undergraduate college that is not a major research institution and hope to be admitted to an experimental psychology or clinical psychology PhD program, do not fret. It is not usually the reputation or size of the school from which you obtain your undergraduate degree that is the most important factor in determining how an admissions committee views your application. Rather, it is what you do during your time as an undergraduate that is often considered more important. Did you excel among the top students in your department or college? Did you get involved in research at your school? If these opportunities were not available to you in your undergraduate program, did you seek out opportunities to be involved in research at other institutions besides your own undergraduate college? These considerations are important if you wish to apply to a graduate program but do not attend an undergraduate program with a strong reputation for research. Remember, admissions committees are looking for applicants who know what they are getting themselves into, are well prepared to embark on graduate studies, are a good match to work with faculty in the program, and have a strong likelihood of succeeding in the program. You can strive to acquire all of these attributes at most undergraduate programs if you are proactive in doing so.

Why You Should Join Clubs and Honor Societies

Colleges often have student organizations such as psychology clubs and psychology honor societies that you can join. These organizations may have GPA and other requirements for joining. Membership in these societies is considered to be an honor and is sometimes even noted on official transcript records as such. Examples of these clubs are Psi Chi (at the 4-year university level) and Psi Beta (at the community college level). Having such a distinction is a positive addition to your list of extracurricular experiences and to your résumé. A more important reason to join than recognition is for the many other types of rewards that these organizations can offer. Both Psi Chi and Psi Beta provide academic recognition and professional growth to their members. Membership also includes benefits such as eligibility for research awards at regional conferences, student grants and awards, subscriptions to newsletters filled with helpful information regarding graduate school and other issues important to undergraduate psychology majors (e.g., *Eye on Psi Chi* quarterly newsletter), and more. Honor societies and clubs promote professional development by bringing in speakers to talk about their own careers in psychology or topics such as academic success, GRE preparation, and other topics relevant to undergraduates in psychology. Honor societies and clubs also foster community service opportunities.

Whether you join an honors or a nonhonors psychology club, you will undoubtedly be exposed to new learning experiences related to psychology, leadership opportunities, and friends who share a common interest—all of which might not have been available to you otherwise. You can not only potentially be exposed to valuable information by joining these organizations, but also attain important leadership skills. If you want to set yourself apart from other graduate school applicants, you should get involved in a leadership role within your honor society or club. Mere membership alone will not necessarily set you apart from other applicants against whom you are competing for a few open slots in a given graduate program. Leadership positions will help you to develop important skills, such as organizational, writing, and speaking skills. These abilities are useful in almost every type of career and can benefit you socially as well.

Speaking of your social life, being a part of an honor society or psychology club allows you to meet other psychology majors with interests similar to yours. Members often network with one another and alumni, use the club to form study groups, compare notes about instructors and classes, and sometimes even investigate potential careers together.

If your school does not have a psychology club or psychology honor society, you may be able to find a club in a related field that can meet these needs (e.g., look for a human development, communications, sociology, or biology student club). Find one that is right for you, and reap the benefits! Go to http://www.psichi.org and http://psibeta.org/site for more information about Psi Chi and Psi Beta, respectively.

How to Research Graduate School Programs

The best place to start when trying to find out which graduate school programs best meet your educational and career goals is the American Psychological Association's (2009) book *Graduate Study in Psychology 2010*. This book can be purchased or may be found in the reference section of your college or university library. This book contains information about over 600 graduate programs, including the number of applications received by a program, number of individuals accepted in each program, dates for applications and admission, types of information required for an application (e.g., GRE scores, letters of recommendations, documentation concerning volunteer or clinical experience), in-state and out-of-state tuition costs, availability of internships and scholarships, employment information of graduates, orientation and emphasis of departments and programs, and more. The American Psychological Association also provides information regarding graduate study as well as many resources for current graduate students at the American Psychological Association for Graduate Students (APAGS) web site (http://www.apa.org/apags/). APAGS offers many resources for current graduate students and even publishes an online magazine geared specifically toward graduate students (*gradPSYCH;* see http://gradpsych.apags.org/). Graduate students who join APAGS have many other resources available to them, including discounted journal subscriptions, the ability to purchase access to PsycINFO, scholarships, internship and career services, listserv subscriptions, and access to liability insurance for graduate students. It may be worthwhile to visit the APAGS web site to learn more about topics and issues that are pertinent to graduate students, even if you are not a current graduate student but considering the prospect of entering graduate school.

You should also ask faculty whom you know for suggestions regarding which graduate school programs might best suit your needs as well as research different programs on your own via the Internet. Carefully read program descriptions and the various faculty members' biographies and consider how many faculty members a program has who specialize in different subdisciplines. This research will give you a good idea of how well represented your chosen subdiscipline is at the prospective school. This datum also is important because it may give you a clue as to whether there would be many resources in terms of potential mentors and funding devoted to that subdiscipline. In addition, it is important to make sure that there are at least one or two faculty members in the program with whom you share common interests and with whom you would like to study.

Of course, in a perfect world, you could be 100% logical in your decision-making process and not factor in variables such as your preference for geographic location when deciding where to apply to graduate school. You will be in graduate school for a limited time, which may provide you a great opportunity to live in a new city. If you are willing to move for a few years rather than staying close to home, then you will have many more options for attending graduate school. However, it would be a waste of time to apply and interview at schools that you would never truly consider attending because of location. See Exhibit 5.2 to learn about how one student found the right graduate school fit.

Can You Contact Faculty at Prospective Graduate Programs?

You should consider contacting faculty members in prospective graduate programs to ask them about their research and whether they plan to take on graduate students in their laboratory in the near future. As long as your interaction with faculty is professional and not seen as an attempt to win them over or unduly influence them, contact is appropriate. You can ask faculty whether they recommend any readings for you that will help you to learn more about their work as well. Consider the following situation as an example of why it is wise to contact a graduate program's faculty members before applying to a graduate program. Suppose you apply to a program and list Professor Jones and Professor Smith as your

EXHIBIT 5.2

One Student's Perspective

Rebecca Hetey, BA, doctoral student, Stanford University
"Finding the Right Graduate School Fit"

Early in my undergraduate career, I did not really know what graduate school was. After a few years of being a psychology major and working in a number of labs alongside graduate students and professors, I gained more insight into what graduate school entailed. In my junior year, as my passion for psychology blossomed and my interests became more refined, I knew that the next step in my career was to apply to doctor of philosophy (PhD) programs in social psychology.

Just as I had not originally known what graduate school was, I was not sure how to go about finding programs to which I could apply. There were so many programs scattered about the country with vastly different philosophies of graduate education and a seemingly infinite number of potential advisors with whom I could work. I needed to start somewhere, so I thought about the authors whose work had inspired me most in terms of the direction my own independent research had taken. I scanned the bibliographies of some of the most personally meaningful papers I had written in college and found that a few professors popped up again and again. Research, I realized, was an ongoing dialogue, an ongoing debate. I wanted my own voice as a scholar to be shaped by those whose voices I found most compelling and most enlightening.

I made a list of these potential advisors and started looking up details of the programs at their home institutions. The Internet has greatly aided in this process, as virtually all psychology graduate programs have very detailed web sites that spell out the admissions requirements and the requirements of the program itself. By examining the information on these web sites, I started to piece together what it would be like to be a student at a particular school.

The process by which you select a graduate school is very different from the process by which you selected an undergraduate institution to attend. Deciding where to apply to college is often largely driven by the overall reputation of the university. The quality of any particular graduate program in a specific field of psychology, however, is not reliably gleaned from the reputation of an entire institution. The best programs might be at universities you might never have heard of, and the most reputable university might not have a strong program. Beyond this consideration, you would likely be unhappy at the best program in the world if it had no professors who shared your research interests and with whom you could work.

I did not know this all-important information when I first started my graduate school search. I quickly realized that to find the proverbial "needle in the haystack" that is the perfect graduate program in psychology, I would need to tap into all of the resources I had at my disposal, including professors with whom I had worked and graduate student mentors whom I met within their laboratories.

They explained to me how graduate students at schools I would be applying to would be important resources for me and instructed me to ask these potential peers about the overall atmosphere of the program, funding issues, living in the area, and how the faculty and students interacted in the program. I was told to specifically seek out and speak with students who worked with the professors I was interested in having as my potential major advisors, as the student–major advisor relationship can have such a great impact on one's graduate school experience.

The time I invested in my careful and thorough search for the best programs to apply to made all the difference when it came time for me to decide which school I would ultimately attend. I had a number of good options from which to choose, and after recently completing my first year of graduate school at Stanford University, I can honestly say that I could not be happier with my choice.

preferred potential major professors (i.e., faculty advisors). Little do you know that Professor Jones is nearing retirement and not taking on new students, and Professor Smith is going on sabbatical the next year and not planning on taking on any new students until the following year. This information would be very useful to have before applying to a program in a particular year. Alternatively, you may apply to this particular program because Professor Jones's biography on the department's web site states that she has published on a specific research topic that greatly interests you. Then you do not learn until meeting her at an official interview that although she is well known for her research on that particular research topic, her laboratory has since shifted its focus to a completely different topic and she no longer conducts research on the topic that initially interested you in her work. There is no way that you could have known any of this information without personally contacting prospective faculty advisors. Contacting faculty members before you apply to graduate programs can save you valuable time and help to inform your decision as to which programs to apply.

Who to Ask for Letters of Recommendation

Most graduate programs require at least three letters of recommendation. It is wise to select letter writers who can speak to your preparedness for graduate studies in their letters of recommendation. Before you ask professors to write a letter of recommendation on your behalf when you apply to a graduate program, consider whether they really know you or whether you are just one of the students in the crowd who earned an "A" in their course. Can they speak to your intelligence, communication skills, organizational abilities, creativity, maturity, knowledge in the field, ability to work well with others, or anything else? It is to your advantage to request letters from professors who know you personally through working with you in a laboratory or internship setting. Your letter of recommendation will be more personal and more informative. (On a side note, it is common practice for professors to collaborate with their graduate students or postdoctoral researchers in writing letters of recommendation on behalf of an undergraduate student if that student actually worked more closely with one of those laboratory members.)

Next, you can ask other professors who know your academic ability, maturity level, and so on to write letters for you. You might want to ask current or past supervisors from related positions that you have held to write a letter. Your letter writers should be able to speak to why you are well prepared to continue your education in psychology at the graduate level. It does not make sense to have a swimming coach write you a letter that says how devoted and hardworking of a person you are in general because this information does not directly address your preparedness or potential to succeed in a psychology graduate program. It is a good idea to set up a short appointment to meet with each of your letter writers and to talk about your goals and education plans. Another helpful step to take is to provide your letter writers with an unofficial copy of your transcripts, a résumé or list of college activities, and/or a short narrative about yourself and your career goals. This information will give them a more well-rounded picture of you as an individual that they can incorporate into their letter along with the usual facts regarding how they know you, how well you performed as a student or worker, and what skills you demonstrated in that capacity.

Be sure to ask for your letters of recommendation well in advance of your application due dates. Four to 6 weeks is a reasonable amount of advance notice to provide a letter writer. If you provide your letter writers a list of graduate schools to which you are applying, be sure to include on that list a bolded, all caps, underlined "**APPLICATION DUE DATE**" next to each graduate school's name. For those schools that do not yet accept electronic applications and request that you submit letters via surface mail, always include stamped, addressed envelopes and any supplemental paperwork or special directions necessary to include with the letter. Do not worry too much about having to ask you letter writers for another letter later on should you decide to apply to another program unexpectedly. They will usually be happy to do so and can simply modify or mail out the original letter that they wrote on your behalf. Be sure to thank them for their help personally with a letter or phone call. It is also considered courteous to keep your letter writers posted on your progress.

What to Include in Your Letter of Intent

The letter of intent is a brief letter of introduction that is included with your application that should include information about your educational and career goals, your academic background, and why you plan to pursue graduate studies. It should be no longer than two typed (single-spaced) pages and should be written clearly and concisely. Be sure to proofread your letter of intent for typos and grammatical errors, as these mistakes will reflect poorly on you as an applicant. There is no strict format for the letter of intent, but there are critical pieces of information that should be included. It should contain a clear statement of your educational and career goals, a brief description of how your interest in your chosen area of psychology developed, a description of your academic history and special skills you may have acquired during your undergraduate years (e.g., statistical skills, computer programming skills, research or clinical skills), how your undergraduate educational or work experiences have led you to pursue graduate studies in the field, and why you have chosen to apply to that particular program.

Although some applications may call the letter of intent an autobiographical or personal statement, it is best to avoid including personal stories that have to do with friends or family members and to keep your letter professional. Avoid stating that you are interested in psychology because you "want to help others," as this statement is cliché and does not speak to your potential or desire to be a research scientist. Faculty members who read your statement of intent are scientists who have devoted their lives to science and academic endeavors and are more likely to want to read about why you are interested in psychology for reasons of scientific curiosity rather than your personal reasons for wishing to pursue a graduate degree. It is appropriate to list the names of faculty members in the potential graduate school program whose research interests match your interests. Be sure that you express your interests so that they are specific enough to show you have seriously considered the program and research area in which you want to work but not so narrow as to make you appear closed minded. The following are some good reference sources to use to help you write your letter of intent.

Books:

- *Getting In: A Step-by-Step Plan for Gaining Admission to Graduate School in Psychology* (American Psychological Association, 2007).
- *Graduate Study in Psychology 2010* (American Psychological Association, 2009).
- *Preparing for Graduate Study in Psychology: 101 Questions and Answers* (Buskist & Burke, 2007).
- *Applying to Graduate School in Psychology: Advice From Successful Students and Psychologists* (Kracen & Wallace, 2008).
- *Insider's Guide to Graduate Programs in Clinical and Counseling Psychology* (Norcross, Sayette, & Mayne, 2008).

Web sites:

- American Psychological Association "A Guide to Getting Into Graduate School" (http://www.apa.org/ed/getin.html).
- The Association for Psychological Science *Observer* online articles (http://www.psychologicalscience.org/observer).

GREs and the Psychology Subject Test

The GRE is a standardized test that is required by almost all graduate programs. This computerized test focuses on measuring abstract thinking skills in the areas of math, vocabulary, and analytical writing. Some graduate programs will also require you to take a specific subject area test in psychology as well. There is no need to get overly nervous about these tests (as many students do) because there are many ways to prepare for them. On each subsection of the exam, there are a finite number of types of questions that you can practice answering. Once you learn strategies for approaching each type of question, you will be ready to handle all of the questions that could possibly be asked on the exam. Free practice GRE exams and access to practice question banks are available at the GRE web site (http://www.ets.org). There are also GRE preparation books and software programs that you can purchase. Check these resources out at your local bookstore. Private companies and some university extension offices also offer GRE preparation classes or workshops. Popular courses are offered by Kaplan Educational Center Ltd. (http://www.kaptest.com), Princeton Review (http://www.princetonreview.come/home.asp), and Number 2 (online only; http://number2.com). Choosing the option to take a prep course is more costly than preparing via books and software, but you should choose the route that is best for you.

You can also find books and software programs to help you prepare for the Psychology Subject Test at bookstores and online. You may also wish to prepare by looking over your old course materials and reviewing a good introductory psychology textbook. According to the GRE web site, the Psychology Subject Test consists of 140 multiple-choice questions, some of which are based on sets of questions related to a description of an experiment or graphs of psychological functions. According to the site, about 40% of questions are experimental or natural science oriented, covering topics including learning, language, memory, thinking, sensation and perception, physiological psychology, ethology, and comparative psychology. About 43% of test questions are social or social science oriented, covering topics including clinical and abnormal, developmental, personality, and social psychology. About 17% of questions are general psychology questions covering topics including the history of psychology, applied psychology, measurement, research designs, and statistics. Practice tests and preparation tips are available at the GRE web site (http://www.ets.org).

What if You Do Not Ace the GRE?

If you do not perform as well as you had hoped on the GRE, you may retake it. You should definitely focus on improving your GRE scores to make your application more competitive, but do not think that all schools treat these scores in the same way. It is true that some schools may use these scores as screening devices to weed out applicants. However, if you do not perform well on the GRE, there are other factors that may outweigh this particular element in your application. First, strong letters of recommendation and research experience can compensate for low GRE scores. In addition, having a faculty member in the program to which you have applied recommend that you be given an interview may overshadow low GRE scores in some cases. A strong statement of intent that reflects your experience and potential to succeed in the program is also important.

If you want to retake the GRE for any reason, you may only do so on certain dates and times of the year (see http://www.ets.org). Be sure to find out whether the graduate school programs to which you are applying will average the scores from multiple attempts of the GRE or will take the highest scores from different attempts. Determining this information should play a role in your decision about whether to retake the GRE and what strategy to use in preparing to retake it. For example, you may perform poorly on the verbal subsection of the GRE and be content with your score on the math subsection. If all the programs to which you are applying take the highest score on each subsection from each attempt, then you can plan to spend most of your preparation time focusing on how to improve your verbal score. However, if the programs to which you are applying take the average of scores on each subsection from multiple attempts, then you should attempt to increase your scores on all subsections of the test. This way, you can avoid potentially lowering your score on one or more subsections as the result of retaking the exam. The graduate program coordinator at prospective graduate school programs should be able to provide the answers to these questions.

What to Do at Your Interviews

If you are invited to a school for an interview, keep in mind that the interview serves a specific purpose for both you and the admissions committee at the prospective program. The program admissions committee wants you to be able to meet with prospective advisors and for both of you to discern whether you would work well together if you were to be offered admission to the program. Second, the committee wants you to get an accurate view of the university, program, its faculty, and its students so that you can make an informed decision should they decide to admit you. As such, the goals of the admissions committee also serve you well. You will have a chance to ask questions and learn as much as you can about the prospective program and your potential faculty mentors in the program while you are there, which should surely help you to make your decision about whether to accept an offer of admission. The best thing you can do is to be yourself, behave professionally throughout the entire visit, be prepared to talk intelligently about what research-related experiences you have had in the past or hope to have in the future, and be ready to show your interest and learn about the program by being prepared to ask questions. In the following sections, we offer several tips on questions that you may wish to consider asking different people while on your visit. These questions are organized into two main categories, those about financial support and those about mentorship available in the program.

QUESTIONS TO ASK ABOUT FINANCIAL SUPPORT

Most PhD programs offer financial support to their students. In some programs, financial support is guaranteed to all students in the program for a certain number of years. In other programs, the amount and guarantee of financial support are tied to the students' major professor (i.e., official advisor of record). In these latter programs, student funding may come from the major professor's grants and not from departmental funds. Master's programs typically do not provide financial support guarantees but may offer opportunities for students to earn money through teaching assistantships and/or research assistantships. The following questions address important funding issues that you should ask program representatives about during your interview:

- How are students supported financially?
- Does the program provide general funding to all students from the same source, or is a student's funding tied to the specific major professor with whom he or she works?
- If funding is provided by the program, are students required to serve as teaching assistants or research assistants as a condition for funding? If so, what is the typical time commitment required for such positions?
- For how many years is funding guaranteed? Does funding typically discontinue after a certain number of years in the program?

- Do students typically receive support in the summer?
- Are paid teaching assistantships or research assistantships available during the summer?
- Where do students obtain funds to attend professional conferences? Do students have to be presenting work at the conference to receive funding?
- Is there subsidized student housing available? If so, is there a waiting list for this housing?

QUESTIONS TO ASK ABOUT FACULTY ADVISORS

The relationship that you have with your faculty advisor (also called major professor) is important, as it can greatly influence your entire graduate school experience. This person is going to be your mentor, your colleague, and your "boss." He or she is going to determine whether you continue in the program by reviewing your performance every year via written report and/or grades and, at least to some extent, determine the course of your career. You will want to ask graduate students or postdoctoral researchers who work with your potential faculty advisor(s) questions to get a sense of what it might be like to work closely with this person. Of course, you should take into account that their answers will reflect their personal experiences and will not necessarily be completely representative of the professor because we all have unique personalities that differentially affect our working relationships with others. However, you can glean a lot of information and see potential red flags easily when asking these questions. The following is a list of potential questions that you might consider tactfully asking graduate students and postdoctoral researchers during your interview:

- What is it like to work for this faculty member?
- Is the faculty member a hands-off supervisor or a micromanager?
- Does the professor provide guidance when needed, or is he or she too busy to mentor students?
- Is the professor pleasant and reasonable to work alongside?
- Does the professor allow students the freedom to develop their own ideas?
- Is credit and authorship assigned to students fairly when it comes to publishing joint research?
- Is the professor eager to publish or slow to publish with students?
- Does the professor give students the freedom to work on their dissertation or thesis projects to complete the degree program in a timely manner?
- Does the professor require students to work on laboratory grant projects that are not related to the students' own publications or graduate work or interests?

MY PROACTIVE PLAN EXERCISES

1. Which potential career paths do I think I would like to consider at this point? Do they require a graduate degree?

2. Does my college or university have a 5th-year master's program? Where did I find the information necessary to answer this question?

3. Is my current grade-point average (GPA) competitive according to the graduate school requirements described in this chapter? If not, is there a chance for me to try to raise it? If so, how do I plan to raise it?

4. Visit my college or university's psychology department web site. View the research interests of the faculty. List at least two faculty members whose research interests me.

5. Visit another college or university's psychology department web site. View the research interests of the faculty. List at least two faculty members whose research interests me.

6. Find out whether my school has a psychology club and/or a Psi Chi or Psi Beta Honor Society in psychology. Which is available at my school? Do I qualify to join? If none are available, what other student organizations might interest me?

7. If I wanted to apply to graduate school, what type of program do I think would best match my interests and why?

8. If I were to apply to graduate school, when would I do so? When would I have to take the GRE in order to apply on time?

9. If I were to ask for letters of recommendation for graduate school, who would I ask? Who would be able to speak to my potential for success as a graduate student? List at least three potential letter writers. When would I have to ask them in order to give them ample time to write my letters?

10. Develop a list of my personal qualities or skills that would be appropriate for me to describe in more detail in my letter of intent. On a point-by-point basis, outline the contents of my letter of intent.

Getting "Real-World" Psychology-Related Experience   6

A s you continue to take courses in psychology and perhaps start to read more about the different psychology career paths that you may wish to consider, it may not be immediately clear to you how the knowledge that you have gained in the classroom relates to potential work settings. In fact, the majority of psychology courses emphasize the teaching of psychological theory and practice rather than emphasizing the connection between psychological theories and their real-world applications outside of academia. The connections are there, of course, but are not always made explicit, which is why being proactive and seeking out opportunities to apply your knowledge and talents in extracurricular activities is so important. You can make connections between classroom material and the real world through firsthand experience as a volunteer or intern in a psychology-related position. In addition, internship, volunteer, and practicum experience can be helpful in making you a desirable candidate for admissions to graduate programs. Many of the skills that you can attain through these sorts of positions may help prepare you for graduate study. In fact, it is highly advised that students applying to clinical psychology or doctor of psychology (PsyD) graduate school programs seek internship, volunteer, and practicum experience in clinical settings before applying.

These experiences will also allow you to try out different job settings and work environments, which is a wonderful way to find out whether a potential line of work, or even working with a particular population, might suit you. As a volunteer or intern, you will also gain valuable skills that can add to your personal and professional development. The many communication, writing, computer, and other skills that you can hone in these positions will undoubtedly be great additions to include on your résumé and graduate school admission applications.

Which Volunteer Positions Suit Psychology Majors Well?

Volunteer positions related to psychology can be found in a wide range of settings. If you are interested in clinical psychology, you may be more interested in a volunteer position related to counseling or psychological health. A volunteer position within a company's human resources department might better suit you if you are considering a career path in industrial–organizational psychology. Volunteering to work with children might be best for psychology majors who want a career in child development. Exhibit 6.1 presents a partial list of settings in which psychology students commonly volunteer.

Most of the types of work settings and organizations listed in Exhibit 6.1 can be found in your local phone book. It takes only a few minutes to place a call and inquire about volunteer possibilities. Because many counties offer such community services, you may also contact your county governance offices to find out whether they have a volunteer placement and referral service, although some colleges even provide this service at their career services center. (Actually your school's career services center may be the best place to start your search for a volunteer position.) Alternatively, you may want to look into using an Internet-based volunteer service to help match you with a site that is seeking volunteers. The following is a partial list of web sites that match volunteer interests with appropriate corresponding organizations:

- *Cool Works volunteerism* (http://www.coolworks.com/volunteer/). This site lists resources that can help you to find a volunteer position and is organized regionally.
- *Global Volunteers* (http://www.globalvolunteers.org). This site offers an international volunteer matching service.
- *Smart Volunteer* (http://www.smartvolunteer.org). This company offers a national volunteer matching service.
- *U.S. Government National Volunteer* (http://www.volunteer.gov/gov/). This site lets you choose your state and find volunteer oppor-

EXHIBIT 6.1

Common Volunteer Settings for Psychology Majors

Hospitals
Day treatment centers for eating disorders
Day treatment centers for substance abuse
Substance abuse treatment centers
Residential facilities for the elderly
Senior centers
Residential facilities for youth
Teen and youth centers
Teen and youth hotlines
Tutoring centers for children
Summer enrichment programs for children
Psychologist–psychiatrist offices
Nonprofit agencies serving the mentally ill and their families (e.g., National Alliance on Mental Illness)
Halfway houses
Shelters for women or children in distress
Support group organizations (e.g., support groups for grieving families)
County social services agencies (e.g., child and family services, helping a case manager)
Private social services agencies (e.g., helping adults or children with disabilities)
Rehabilitation centers for those who have suffered stroke or other brain injury
Research laboratories within colleges (see Chapter 5) or companies
District attorney's offices
HIV prevention programs
Alcohol abuse prevention programs on college campuses
Student health advocacy groups on college campuses
Domestic abuse prevention programs

tunities in your own area that are sponsored by different government agencies.

- *Volunteer Match* (http://www.volunteermatch.org). This site offers a national volunteer matching service.

In addition, you may wish to consult Silvia, Delaney, and Marcovitch's (2009) book to learn more about the kinds of activities you may wish to participate in as an undergraduate psychology major.

Is a Volunteer Position Right for You?

There are some important things to keep in mind before taking on the responsibility and commitment involved with volunteer positions. First, most volunteer positions are not paid and are not meant to lead to paying positions. If you need to spend your time outside of school earning money, take this point into account and consider finding a part-time job or paid internship related to psychology instead.

Second, before you agree to take on a position, be sure to ask questions about the time commitment involved. Does the organization require a certain minimum number of hours per week from its volunteers? How much of a long-term commitment would you be making by taking on this position? Time commitments can vary widely from one position to another. For example, volunteer positions such as assisting with a field research project or an ongoing support group require a lengthier time commitment than perhaps assisting with a summer camp program. They both require lengthy training and repeated meetings over a longer period of time. Assess your existing time commitments and ask yourself how much time you have available each week and whether you can stick with a volunteer position over the long term.

Third, you should also ask for a description of the expected duties required in the volunteer position. It is important to make sure that at least some of the required duties will allow for you to gain the type of experience that you seek to achieve as a volunteer. For example, if you hope to learn more about behavior analysis by working closely with animals and trainers as a volunteer at a zoo, you will want to be sure that at least some of your volunteer duties involve this kind of experience. What a shame it would be to find out that your duties were far from working with the actual animals or observing trainers but included instead only cleaning up after animals or interacting with zoo patrons. Being clear about what you are signing on for before you start will help ensure that you enjoy your volunteer position and get the type of experience that you want. Read more about one student's experience volunteering in a clinical setting in Exhibit 6.2.

What Is the Difference Between a Volunteer Position and an Internship?

A volunteer position is more loosely defined than an internship position and does not involve any sort of compensation or educational component. Internships are usually work or service opportunities with an educational component and typically involve clearly defined projects and goals, a set time frame, and possible pay. Student interns gain professional experience related to their major or career goal in an occupational area

---

EXHIBIT 6.2

One Student's Perspective

Annie H., BS, doctoral candidate in clinical psychology, University of California, San Diego
"Why I Am Glad I Volunteered in a Clinical Psychology Setting"

As an undergraduate psychology major, I wanted to be a clinical psychologist, but I was not sure what area of clinical psychology to select as my specialty. I decided to serve as a volunteer in the Family Mental Health Program at the local Veteran's Affairs hospital. My duties did not involve counseling people, of course, but I was in an environment that allowed me to learn much about what life as a clinical psychologist might be like.

I am glad I volunteered because it helped to solidify my decision to pursue a graduate degree in clinical psychology and to choose my specialty research and clinical area of couple therapy. As a volunteer, I got the opportunity to work with couple therapists with different types of training, including doctoral-level psychologists, psychology interns, marital and family therapists, and marriage and family therapist trainees. I got to see what they did firsthand by participating in clinical roundtable meetings and viewing videotapes of therapy sessions in which I could watch couple therapists in action. Volunteering at this site allowed me to learn about different models and frameworks of couple therapy, network with clinical psychologists and other professionals, assist in conducting couple relationship research, and show graduate school admissions committees that I was serious about becoming a psychologist.

---

they are considering. An internship usually involves working in a professional setting under the guidance and supervision of practicing professionals. For this reason, working as an intern is a great way to "test drive" possible careers and pick up directly marketable skills. An internship usually requires a level of responsibility that allows a student to develop new skills.

Internships can be paid (via salary or stipend) or unpaid and can sometimes be incorporated into the college curriculum for course credit. Although some students might be less than thrilled to work for no pay, some employers use internships as a way to test out potential employees. Whether this is company policy or not, your experience within an organization can give you an edge over other applicants when you later apply for positions within the organization.

An internship provides students with the opportunity to gain skills that will make them more marketable in the workforce and may lead to valuable professional contacts. Internships also are a useful way for recent graduates to bridge the gap between school and the professional world. Internships provide students with a sense of how the work world differs from the academic world. Interns learn about the inner workings of an organization and about the work schedules, duties, and roles of professionals within it, which is valuable knowledge for students who may not have had much work experience within an organization or company. Internships can also benefit students who are already in the workforce but are considering changing careers and are not ready to make a permanent commitment. Internship listings can usually be found posted in all of the same places that similar employment opportunities are posted. You may wish to check whether your college career services center has separate listings of internships or even an internship placement program. Popular job search sites also list internship opportunities. For example, check out the following web sites:

- http://www.monster.com
- http://www.careerbuilder.com
- http://www.jobsearchusa.org
- http://www.jobs.com
- http://www.indeed.com

A few other popular online sites that provide a multitude of internship listings in different fields are as follows:

- http://www.internjobs.com
- http://www.internshipprograms.com
- http://www.job-hunt.org/interns.shtml
- http://www.wetfeet.com

To read about how an internship helped shape one professional's career and how a volunteer position helped form the basis of one student's career decisions, read Exhibits 6.3 and 6.4.

How Can You Make the Most of Your Volunteer Position or Internship on Paper?

Serving as a volunteer or an intern for an organization speaks to what kind of person you are to employers and graduate schools considering your application. It suggests that you are a person who takes initiative, seeks to learn, and desires to serve others. It also implies that you have gained skills that are relevant to the professional world. In fact, experience as a volunteer or intern can serve as a foot in the door to achieving your first paid position in the workforce if you are someone who otherwise lacks past work experience. After you have served as a volunteer or intern within an organization for some period of time, it is both appropriate and beneficial for you to include a description of this experience on your résumé and/or graduate school application. You can describe volunteer work on your résumé by listing the organization's name and location, your functional title, the dates of your work, your

EXHIBIT 6.3

One Professional's Perspective

Michelle Donovan, PhD, People Analytics Team Member at Google, Inc.
"A Fulfilling Career in Industrial–Organizational Psychology"

During my doctoral program, I was selected for internship at a company called Personnel Decisions Research Institutes in Washington, DC, that consisted of two major projects. The first was to help design a survey to measure adaptability and administer it at several Army bases. The data that we collected resulted in an award-winning paper presented at the annual meeting of the Society of Industrial/Organizational Psychology (SIOP; http://www.siop.org). It was really gratifying to be recognized in front of the more than 3,000 attendees. Our second project was conducting a job analysis at a government agency in which we conducted interviews, studied people's jobs, and trained them on computer software, which helped them describe their jobs. It was during this internship that I fell in love with the idea of working as an industrial–organizational (I/O) psychologist in an applied setting. When I returned to Illinois to finish my doctorate, there was no turning back. I wanted to finish my dissertation, get my doctorate, and start working in this field.

My first job after my doctorate was at a small consulting firm in the San Francisco Bay area called Terranova Consulting Group. At Terranova, I worked on a wide variety of projects—a training needs analysis survey for a biotech company; human resource audits for startups in the Silicon Valley; and job analysis projects for various companies to help them understand what their people did and how to select, train, develop, and manage them in those jobs. I found the projects that I enjoyed most were organizational surveys. The idealist in me loved the idea that I could capture "the voice of the people," apply some unique skills (analyzing the data and creating a presentation to tell the story), and then convince leaders to take action to improve the work environment based on the data. So when I saw an opening at Intel Corporation called "survey researcher," which involved managing surveys full time, I decided to have an informational interview with them to learn more. That informational interview turned into a job offer, and I spent the next several years at Intel working on surveys, focus groups, and other projects related to human resource data and metrics to help inform important decisions and strategies (e.g., How do we retain people? What should our company look like in the future?).

After 6 years at Intel, I moved on and found my next job at Google through a person I met networking. I have been with Google for 2 years now, where I am part of a team called People Analytics. Although Google's mission is to organize the world's information and make it universally accessible and useful, the mission of People Analytics is to organize information on Google users and make it accessible and useful to our leaders, managers, and in some cases to Googlers themselves (as Google employees are called). Our goal is to ensure that all people-related decisions are based on data—not an easy task because we make hundreds of people-related decisions a day.

My specific role is to manage our survey program, which includes our annual survey sent worldwide to over 20,000 Googlers. I also manage a small team that helps collect and analyze data, such as surveys and focus groups (we call them "roundtables" at Google so they do not sound scary and people actually show up). Our group is responsible for not merely gathering the data, but also for making sure that data influences change—real and meaningful change. After just 3 months at Google, I made recommendations based on some data I analyzed, and when I presented to two directors, they said, "Yes, do it!" In moments like that, I feel a part of something very special—helping to make Google a better place to work. Granted, some of the changes our data has led to are small (e.g., new fitness courses based on a fitness survey), but

(Continued)

EXHIBIT 6.3 (*Continued*)

some are bigger and more far reaching (a much greater emphasis on career development for Googlers and fundamental changes in the compensation and benefits we offer).

Over the years and ever since that first internship, I have had the privilege of studying many different kinds of jobs, including assembly line workers, salespeople, soldiers, security guards, ordnance officers, analysts, managers, software and hardware engineers, chefs, and chief executive officers. What I know for sure is that although every job is unique and fulfilling in its own way, the job of an I/O psychologist is still the best fit for me.

EXHIBIT 6.4

One Student's Perspective

Tannia Henetz, BA, doctoral student, Stanford University
"How Volunteering as an Undergraduate Teaching Assistant Helped Me"

During my years as an undergraduate psychology student, I tried to take advantage of all the opportunities my major had to offer: courses and seminars, research positions, and organizations such as Psi Chi. However, of all my adventures in psychology, I look back with special fondness on the time I spent volunteering as an undergraduate teaching assistant (TA). I loved being a TA, and after my first time doing it, I found myself assisting with multiple courses in some capacity or another from spring of my sophomore year to graduation. The courses were all quite different from one another, and the experience never became tiresome. Each new subject or group of students brought new challenges and perspectives. Teaching—yes, good moments and bad, stresses and rewards—added a dimension to my studies that both enhanced and complemented my other adventures in psychology, and I wholeheartedly recommend that you consider trying it yourself. One unexpected benefit of being a TA was interpersonal in nature. It offered the opportunity and great satisfaction of spending time with people who shared my interests and goals. I will always be grateful to have found, in those opportunities, a group of truly exceptional instructors and graduate student TAs who served as inspiration and eventually became my mentors, colleagues, and good friends. The dedication to teaching that I witnessed during those sessions was simply infectious.

When you are a TA, you learn a lot! First, you are exposed to the ins and outs of teaching a course. You might prepare materials, class web sites, and readings; collaborate to write and grade tests; and hold office hours, sections, and/or review sessions. You also form a deeper understanding of the material you are presenting in class. If you get to give a lecture—fear of suffering humiliation while in the front of a lecture hall full of people is not the only motivator for increased understanding, but it helps—your insights will expand beyond the limits of your own introspection as you respond to the collective curiosity of all your students.

Serving as a TA was also an excellent way for me to explore, and ultimately prepare for, potential career paths after graduation. I was considering graduate school with an eye toward a future in academia. However, how could I be sure my chosen path would actually suit my talents and interests? I needed experience. I set out to try as many of the activities I expected to encounter in my graduate career as I could, particularly research and teaching. As an undergraduate TA, I got a glimpse of my potential future in graduate school and felt more informed when the time came to make my decision about life after college. There is no denying that teaching is a welcome addition to a résumé or curriculum vita, regardless of what you plan to do with your psychology degree. Teaching experience demonstrates responsibility, a collaborative ethic, and the ability to communicate ideas successfully to a wide audience—all pluses for a future employer or adviser.

supervisor's name and contact information, and a description of your duties. Of course, be sure to indicate that you served as a volunteer if that is not clearly indicated by the functional title you provide.

Merely including the dates and title of your position is not enough to ensure that employers and graduate schools get an adequate picture of you and the talents that you may have developed or demonstrated as a volunteer or intern. You should take the time to craft your résumé and applications so that the specific skills that you acquired or practiced in your position are highlighted. You need to present your volunteer or internship experience in a way that will have the most impact on your résumé or graduate school applications.

When writing a résumé or describing your experience in a graduate school application, it is best to use action verbs that accurately reflect the skills and duties involved in your volunteer or intern position. Action verbs are great to use in résumés and applications because they capture interest, have a stronger impact on the reader than passive wording, and more accurately reflect your experience. For example, if you were to list on your résumé that you were a "teen hotline volunteer," you may simply write, "Responsibilities included: answering phone calls and increasing teen hotline calls." However, this description is not specific enough to show that you gained experience in counseling, making decisions independently, and leading others to a successful outcome. It would be more powerful and better reflect these skills if you described your duties as follows:

> Responsibilities included: answered hotline calls, counseled teens in noncrisis situations, screened calls for crisis situations and determined whether callers should be referred for professional help, and planned and led a campaign to increase hotline awareness that resulted in a 20% call increase.

You can see that the use of more descriptive action verbs, the past tense, and specifics (e.g., the percentage increase in calls) in the revised description of duties gets across much more information about what you actually did and achieved in your volunteer role than the original version.

As you read in Chapter 5, there are specific characteristics and qualities that graduate schools generally seek in applicants. The same is true of employers: Some of the qualities that employers value are those skills that graduate programs value as well (e.g., oral and written communication skills, motivation, organizational skills; see Chapter 5 for further discussion). In preparing to write your own résumé and application materials, you should identify not only the skills related to the specific job or graduate program to which you are applying, but also the general positive qualities you possess as an individual. Table 6.1 presents the general qualities that many employers who hire psychology graduates find appealing in an applicant. In the right-hand column, you will find

TABLE 6.1

Desirable Qualities in Job Applicants and Related Action Verbs

Desirable quality	Related action verbs
Public speaking	Briefed, communicated, informed, lectured, persuaded, presented, proposed, showed
Communication— interpersonal and written	Advised, assembled, briefed, clarified, communicated, composed, condensed, constructed, counseled, demonstrated, directed, documented, drafted, edited, facilitated, illustrated, informed, interpreted, negotiated, persuaded, presented, proposed, prepared, qualified, reviewed, revised, resolved, simplified
Writing (reports and proposals)	Briefed, clarified, compiled, defined, generated, informed, interpreted, maintained, modified, summarized, submitted, synthesized, translated, verified, wrote
Statistics, mathematical reasoning, and computer skills	Analyzed, balanced, budgeted, calculated, classified, compared, computed, estimated, evaluated, examined, formulated, financed, gathered, integrated, interpreted, measured, mapped, observed, obtained, predicted, processed, projected, quantified, questioned, recorded, reinforced, researched, studied, summarized, tabulated, tested
Teamwork skills	Assisted, collaborated, counseled, empowered, encouraged, enforced, facilitated, guided, helped, instructed, motivated, participated, oversaw, represented, resolved, reinforced, served, supported
Motivation	Achieved, acted, administered, applied, assembled, attained, built, completed, conducted, constructed, coordinated, created, demonstrated, earned, improved, introduced, invented, met, realized, received, repaired, solved, undertook, spearheaded, utilized
Flexibility	Adapted, improvised, learned, introduced, invented, modified, took over, undertook
Ability to think independently and make decisions	Administered, allocated, assessed, averted, classified, conceptualized, consolidated, controlled, decided, defined, determined, developed, devised, diagnosed, eliminated, identified, implemented, initiated, innovated, installed, realized, performed, proposed, questioned, produced, repaired, verified
Organizational skills	Arranged, collected, coordinated, identified, improved, maintained, organized, planned, streamlined, synthesized, systematized, simplified
Leadership skills	Empowered, encouraged, advised, coached, conducted, counseled, controlled, coordinated, directed, guided, handled, headed, instituted, led, managed, motivated, monitored, oversaw, planned, realized, showed, supervised, taught, trained, undertook, served, staffed, supported

Note. Data from Edwards and Smith (1988), Appleby (1997), DeGalan and Lambert (1995), Lock (1988), and Kuther (2003).

action verbs related to each of the general desirable qualities presented on the left. The goal is to choose the words that best describe how you demonstrated the desirable qualities in the left column as a volunteer, intern, or employee in your résumé, graduate school application, or job application.

An activity is included in the "My Proactive Plan Exercises" worksheet at the end of this chapter that is aimed at helping you learn to prepare your own résumé, graduate school application, or job application in a way that best highlights your talents and abilities. The first part of the activity requires that you to consider the general desirable qualities of an applicant presented in Table 6.1. You should list all relevant experiences that you have had as a volunteer, intern, or employee that required or reflected these qualities. You also may use this worksheet to help you describe your other extracurricular activities as well (e.g., club memberships, research assistantships). For the second part of this exercise, you should list the actual duties that you performed in your position (e.g., filing case documents, attending meetings, working on a database, helping individuals). After completing this task, you will then list these same duties and experiences and choose some appropriate action verbs to best describe your role in completing these activities. Completing the entire exercise will put you well on your way to drafting a successful résumé, graduate school application, or job application.

MY PROACTIVE PLAN EXERCISES

1. List five volunteer settings that interest me from Exhibit 6.1 and explain why. Put a star next to the volunteer setting that interests me most.
2. Choose at least one web site from the list of web sites that is oriented toward connecting volunteers with organizations in need of volunteers. List at least two volunteer positions I found on the site that interest me.
3. If I were to take on a volunteer position, how much time per month do I realistically have to devote to it? What days of the week would I be available?
4. Does my college or university offer course credit for internships? If so, what sort of educational benefit do I hope to acquire while working as an intern?
5. Visit one of the web sites provided in this chapter that lists internship opportunities. List at least two internship postings that seem interesting to me and explain why.
6. Does my college or university offer course credit for internship work?
7. Create a two column list and write down all relevant internship, volunteer, or job experiences that I have had (or hope to have) that

would allow me to demonstrate the qualities listed in Table 6.1. Write the relevant quality on the left-hand column and corresponding position–experience on the right-hand column.

8. Create another two-column list and on the left side, write down the actual duties that I performed in each of these internships or volunteer positions I mentioned in my answer to item 7. Then, on the right side, list action verbs from Table 6.1 that I could use to describe my activities on a résumé, graduate school application, or job application.

Psychology Careers in Research and Practice

7

A s you have learned by reading this book, many psychology majors initially choose to major in psychology out of an interest in helping people. Actually, only about half of psychologists make their living by helping individuals on a day-to-day basis. You will recall from Chapter 3 that professional psychologists can be separated into two major categories: academic and applied psychologists. Academic psychologists typically are involved in research and/or teaching. Applied psychologists include those individuals who practice psychology or otherwise apply psychological knowledge in real-world settings. Of course, there are applied psychologists who conduct research as well (e.g., clinical psychologists may provide therapy as well as conduct research). Applied psychologists work in settings that vary from public and private agencies to clinical practice. In fact, the businesses of professional clinical psychologists and other professionals who focus on helping individuals with their psychological well-being are often called psychology "practices."

If you decide that you want to have a career in psychology, you will need to pursue the necessary training to attain your specific career goals. There are two distinct educational tracks that prepare one to work as a research psychologist (in academia or other settings) or as a practitioner. For this reason, you will most likely need to choose between these two general tracks early in your education or at least before applying to graduate training programs. In this chapter, we provide you with an overview of job-related activities and career profiles for various research and practice careers. We also provide you with some self-assessment exercises to help you in your decision-making process.

Academia

Psychologists who work as professors at academic institutions are considered to work in "academia." Although all professors work in academia, professorial duties can vary greatly between academic institutions. One major reason for this is because some institutions are more teaching oriented, and others are more research oriented.

PROFESSORS AT TEACHING-ORIENTED COLLEGES

Not all college professors conduct research. Those professors who work at teaching-oriented colleges are not always required to do so. Teaching-oriented colleges can be 4-year liberal arts colleges or 2-year community colleges. The teaching load is usually heavier at 2-year institutions, where there are little or no research demands on faculty, relative to 4-year institutions. Some 4-year teaching-oriented institutions expect faculty to devote some time to research. However, the research demands placed on faculty at these institutions are generally much lighter than what is required of faculty at research-oriented institutions. College professors who work at research-oriented institutions are required to conduct original research and publish research reports in scientific journals. They teach fewer undergraduate courses because they devote a large proportion of their time to research activities, including training graduate students to conduct research. Conversely, faculty members at teaching-oriented colleges are expected to focus the majority of their time on teaching courses and interacting with undergraduates. Such professors may have a master's degree, but most hold doctoral degrees.

Professors at teaching-oriented colleges have various duties related to teaching, such as developing lesson plans, lecturing and other forms of class presentations, responding to students' learning needs, grading–evaluating student work, and reading and attending conferences to stay abreast of their field. They also serve on college committees that deal with policies having to do with academics, curriculum, budget, hiring, and so forth. The benefits of being a professor at a teaching-oriented college can be both personal and practical. Many such professors enjoy the intellectually stimulating environment of their work setting and having colleagues who also truly enjoy their subject matter. The majority of them find it personally rewarding to share their love of the field with their students. Most professors at teaching-oriented colleges also have flexible schedules in which they have a set number of hours that they are required to be in the classroom or in regularly scheduled office hours but are able to decide how to allocate the rest of their time to professional duties. Some of the practical benefits of being a faculty member at a teaching-oriented college have to do with job availability, security, and expectations. There are many more academic positions available at teaching-oriented institutions than at research-oriented institutions. Most teaching-oriented colleges grant tenure, a special status of job security for faculty, after several requirements have been met over a period of years. Tenure requirements differ among institutions but focus primarily on excellence in teaching. Finally, professors at teaching-oriented colleges are less likely to feel the pressure that many professors at research-oriented institutions feel to conduct large amounts of research. You can read about one professor's account of her career working at a teaching-oriented college in Exhibit 7.1.

PROFESSORS AT RESEARCH-ORIENTED COLLEGES

Faculty at research-oriented institutions hold doctoral degrees and conduct research in their specialty area within psychology. In running their laboratories, many of these professors write applications for grants to fund their research. This sort of writing is time consuming: Grant writing is a recurrent process that often requires the writing of periodic progress reports after grants have been awarded as well as the continual writing of grant renewal applications.

Some benefits to being a professor at a research-oriented institution include a flexible schedule, high levels of intellectual stimulation through research and interaction with colleagues, personal satisfaction from researching interesting topics, and professional satisfaction from generating new psychological knowledge. Psychologists who are self-driven and have a high degree of curiosity are likely to be most fulfilled in this type of position. Another potential benefit of working as a professor at a research-oriented college is the ability to achieve job security after earning tenure. Tenure requirements differ among institutions but usually involve meeting high expectations related to research productivity.

Some challenges also exist for individuals who desire to become professors at research-oriented institutions. Because teaching-oriented colleges outnumber research-oriented colleges, there is a lot of competition for the relatively few research positions that open up each year at research-oriented schools. For example, if your area of research is social

One Professional's Perspective

Kathryn Damm, PhD, Assistant Professor at Nevada State College
"A Career at a Teaching-Oriented College"

In my second year of college, I was on the path to become an elementary school teacher. I enrolled in a social psychology course that changed my future forever. I fell in love with the course and knew at that moment that I wanted to be a psychology researcher. When I speak to my students now, I remind them of the benefit of taking a variety of classes. Most students groan at the general education requirements, but I encourage students to embrace these experiences. You may discover a love for a new topic. I am certainly glad I opted to take social psychology that semester.

It was perfect timing because a graduate student posted an announcement for an "honors" student to be her research assistant. I volunteered and started running studies under her mentorship the next semester. I worked closely with this graduate student and learned so much about the field's opportunities. This experience was invaluable. I encourage those "go-getter" students to pursue working closely with a graduate student or faculty member. You learn far more about what the field has to offer than any class or book could share. One of the biggest selling points for me was the fact that her tuition was being paid and she was given a monthly income by the university to be a graduate student. (These stipends are often paid for being a teaching assistant or working as a research assistant.) The idea of going to graduate school so I could do more research of my own while getting paid and having my tuition covered was very appealing; I thought, "Sign me up!"

While in graduate school, I discovered that my first career goal of teaching was not as far off as I had thought. I love teaching. I enjoy working with students and finding new ways to help them master the material. I often find myself standing in front of my class acting like a monkey or shouting like a victim to help get my points across. In fact, at the start of every semester, I lose about 10 pounds because of my increased activity level while teaching. Perhaps I have discovered a new dieting trend.

I discovered that the best way to get started in a teaching career in psychology was to pick up as many part-time teaching positions as possible at area community colleges. I was lucky that there were many of these colleges in my area. The system only allows you to teach three to four classes at each college. There were many of us "freeway fliers" who would teach three to four classes at three to four colleges. The positions paid well compared with our graduate school stipends, but part-time teaching was not an ideal setup long term. For example, most part-timers do not get health benefits and there is no guarantee from semester to semester that you will have courses to teach.

Eventually, I applied to full-time positions at community colleges and teaching institutions. I still really enjoyed doing my research, but I wanted to be at an institution that valued teaching. My goal was to end up at a 4-year college that focused on teaching but supported research as well. If I could not find that position, I planned to seek community college positions and to supplement this experience with my own research.

Fortunately, I landed the job of my dreams at Nevada State College. Nevada State College is a relatively new 4-year college that focuses on teaching but embraces research as well. In fact, when on the job market, I, and many of my friends, often felt discouraged because of the heavy competition, low number of jobs, and specificity of available positions. Teaching at Nevada State College is exactly what I wanted and more. I have small class sizes, so I get to know my students. And, let me say, I really know my students. I know their personalities, their family dynamics, their barriers to education, and their personal commitments to learn. Teaching is rewarding for many reasons. It is rewarding because of the attention you receive at the

EXHIBIT 7.1 *(Continued)*

front of a room. In turn, the rewards from paying attention to your students can be far greater. When I taught a 300+ person class at the University of California, San Diego, my jokes made the room roar and the hair on my arm stand up. I felt very powerful, not to mention funny. In a 40 person class, my jokes are still funny, yet the roar is not as loud. However, I feel more empowered by the student who comes to my office for help and leaves understanding a difficult topic.

I still get to conduct research while teaching four classes each semester. I have students helping me with studies about teaching techniques, social psychological theories, and so forth. We have a blast working together doing research, and I still have as much fun doing research as that first day as an undergraduate so many years ago. I am thrilled when I see eager young students of my own fall in love with research and look forward to the day that my first undergraduate student tells me that they have also fallen in love with teaching, as I did.

I enjoy my position because every day is fun and exciting for me. I enjoy teaching college students who are eager to learn and who contribute to my own understanding of the material on a regular basis. I have to add, though, that an important feature to enjoying my position is that the flexible schedule gives me the time I need to be an involved mother. I am encouraged to bring my 4-year-old to work when possible, and my hours are flexible. I pick her up from school every day and have plenty of time to visit parks, make dinner, play games, read books, and so on. This semester, for example, my classes do not begin until the afternoon, so I volunteer in her classroom a few mornings a week. I believe that long-term happiness in a position is made from two essential components: loving what you do and flexibility for the other things in your life. If I no longer needed to work to earn money, I would still continue teaching at Nevada State College out of pure enjoyment.

For all of you who are also looking for the career that will be personally rewarding to you, please feel free to look me up at Nevada State College and contact me anytime to ask questions about my career experiences.

psychology, there may be only 10 to 15 positions open around the country in a given year for college professors conducting social psychological research. Research professors often increase their chances of finding a full-time position if they are willing to move far away from home and/or out of state. Still, there are usually over 100 applicants or more per position, so the competition is usually tough. Many applicants make themselves more competitive on the job market by spending a few years after earning their doctorate working as a postdoctoral researcher at either an academic institution or other research setting (e.g., medical school). In fact, postdoctoral experience is typical now among individuals applying for positions as college professors at research institutions, meaning that the road to landing such a position may be a long one. Those individuals who envision themselves conducting cutting-edge research and contributing to the world's knowledge about psychology as psychology professors at research-oriented schools should consider these factors to have a realistic view of the road ahead.

Research Careers
in the Private Sector

Psychological research can have many practical applications, as evidenced by the need for researchers in the private sector (i.e., industry and other nonacademic arenas, including government agencies and nonprofit organizations). Researchers in the private sector usually hold at least a master's degree and often hold a doctoral degree. Individuals who hold master's degrees are usually not in senior positions and instead conduct research themselves, whereas those individuals who hold doctoral degrees are more likely to be in senior positions that involve directing or supervising research projects. Accordingly, researchers working in industry who hold a doctorate are compensated more than researchers with master's degrees.

Just as college professors at research-oriented colleges may research different topics depending on their area of expertise, so do researchers working in the private sector. They may work in many different settings, including pharmaceutical companies, high-tech companies, consulting firms, health care companies, large corporations, and private and public agencies. Companies hire psychology researchers who conduct research on human behavior as it relates to their specific industries and products. For example, knowledge of how users perceive and use products is critical to creating optimal product design. A researcher who specializes in cognitive psychology may be employed by a software firm or telecommunications firm to investigate the interaction between consumers and their computer and telecommunication products. This sort of research falls into the category of human factors psychology. Visit http://www.mypsychmentor.com to read about applied psychology careers in forensic psychology, sports psychology, statistical consulting, industrial–organizational psychology, and more. To learn more about one individual's career in applied psychology, see Exhibit 7.2.

GENERAL JOB ACTIVITIES OF RESEARCHERS

The duties of a researcher may differ depending on the level of one's position within an organization as well as the specific field of psychological study. There are many researchers whose positions require them to be involved in the day-to-day activities of conducting research. These duties may include working alone or with others to collect data, analyzing data using computer and statistical software, writing reports, and giving presentations about their findings. More senior-level researchers may be involved with the planning and management of research projects. These researchers may design studies, train other research personnel to perform data collection, and oversee the progress of multiple projects. Senior-level

EXHIBIT 7.2

One Professional's Perspective

Lawrence Najjar, PhD, Interaction Designer, TandemSeven
"A Career in Human Factors Psychology"

I design software so that it is easy to use. My job has a lot of different names—human factors engineer, usability specialist, information architect, user experience architect, and engineering psychologist. The name that seems to be the best match right now is interaction designer.

I received a master's degree in engineering psychology from the Georgia Institute of Technology. My first job was for a government contractor outside of Washington, DC. I designed a software and hardware user interface to help government analysts translate intercepted foreign language audio messages into English text. I talked to a user representative and wrote detailed specifications that described how I wanted the user interface to work.

My next job was with IBM. I helped design the user interface for the next generation of U.S. air traffic controllers. I observed and talked to air traffic controllers around the country. One lesson I learned is that you cannot count on users to tell you what to design. The few users with opinions only asked for the new system to work faster than their current system. After the user-analysis phase, I performed trade-off studies and designed a customized keyboard, selected a new trackball, designed the audio alerts, worked on the design of new digital flight strips, helped with the ergonomics of the workstation, and designed an efficient layout of workstations in the en-route centers.

After that project, I moved to the commercial side of IBM in Atlanta and mostly did usability tests of software products. The software was designed by programmers rather than people like me, who focus on the needs of the prospective users. It showed. I asked representative users to perform typical tasks using early versions of software. I listed the many problems the users had, rated the usability severity, and suggested design solutions.

I then went back to Georgia Tech to get my PhD. It was supposed to take 2 years, but it took over 5 years. I worked part time on campus at the Georgia Tech Research Institute writing design requirements for highway traffic management center operators, performing an accessibility evaluation on an advanced photocopier, and designing and evaluating a wearable computer user interface for poultry plant quality inspectors. For the wearable computer, we used a head-mounted display, simple voice recognition, ear-protecting headphones with speakers for audio feedback, and a very simple application that I designed. Our prototype worked perfectly in a test run in an actual plant.

Then the World Wide Web happened, and I wanted to be part of that user interface revolution. I got into a couple of web design firms and worked on AOL's online annual report, Home Depot's first e-commerce store, the redesign of NASCAR.com, and a wide variety of other projects. The dot-com boom went bust, my company died, and I was laid off. I could not get a permanent, full-time job for 18 months.

My current job is with a 40-person design consulting firm called TandemSeven. The world has gone web. So, I mostly design portals for company intranets and complex, browser-based applications. My clients include Abbott Laboratories, Campbell Soup Company, Girl Scouts of America, and Orbitz Worldwide. I get to use my years of experience to work smart and fast. I do a wide variety of work, including writing proposals, presenting proposals to prospective clients, learning new domains, interviewing users to identify their needs, creating personas that describe users with representative needs, writing prioritized design requirements, working with clients, performing iterative user interface design, conducting quick usability evaluations, and writing detailed design specifications. The projects last several months, and each one is different. I feel like I am using a lot of my brain.

A career in interaction design may be right for you if the more you learn about it, the more you think, "Wow. That is so cool." Visit http://www.mypsychmentor.com for my advice on how to start a career in human factors psychology.

researchers commonly spend more time managing and writing about research projects than actually conducting the research on their own.

The outlook for research careers in the private sector is good. In particular, there has been significant growth in areas such as human–computer interaction, software development, product usability, marketing research, and industrial–organizational psychology in recent years.

SELF ASSESSMENT: IS RESEARCH RIGHT FOR YOU?

Here are some questions that you can ask yourself to determine whether you might be well suited for a career in research.

- Am I a naturally inquisitive person who often asks why things happen to occur?
- Do I truly enjoy the process of solving puzzles? Or, do I become easily flustered and give up?
- Am I a patient person? Does it take a lot to frustrate or discourage me?
- Do I enjoy reading and learning?
- Do I get excited when I learn about new research findings?
- Do I enjoy reading journal articles?
- Do I like giving presentations?
- Do I enjoy writing?
- Can I handle criticism of my work?
- Do I enjoy planning long-term projects?
- Am I willing to spend at least 5 years in graduate school preparing for a research career?
- Am I a person with high perseverance?
- Would I be good at managing personnel or students?
- Am I willing to move myself and possibly my family for my career if necessary?
- Am I self-driven and highly motivated?
- Can I make my own work schedule and stick to it?

If you answered "yes" to many or most of these questions, then you may be well suited for a career in research. The last three questions are especially relevant to anyone who is considering a career in research.

Careers Related to the Practice of Psychology

As mentioned earlier, there are many types of careers that involve the practice, or application, of psychology. Many psychology majors envision themselves working in these types of careers. As discussed in Chapter 3, clinical psychologists are licensed psychologists who hold a doctoral degree. Clinical psychology degree programs train individuals to apply therapeutic techniques to help individuals who suffer from negative psychological or emotional issues. However, it is not only bona fide clinical psychologists who can work in careers that involve helping others. Social workers, marriage and family therapists, counselors, and other professionals can help individuals on a day-to-day basis in their work. To read more about why one student chose the practice path over the research path, see Exhibit 7.3.

EXHIBIT 7.3

One Student's Perspective

Holly Forman, BA (Psychology), MA (Counseling Psychology, Marriage and Family Therapy), University of San Francisco

"Why I Chose the Counseling Psychology–Marriage and Family Therapy Path"

I majored in psychology at San Diego State University. I was interested in the research side of psychology and worked with Dr. Jim Sallis on how the environment affects physical activity. I even published an article as an undergraduate. During the last year of my degree, I contemplated what area of psychology I wanted to work in for my master's degree. However, after seeing what a lengthy process was involved with research and how tedious it could be, I decided that I did not want to focus on research and was more interested in working with clients in the mental health field. However, narrowing it down this far was not enough. There were still so many directions that I could take and different kinds of graduate programs I could consider.

I researched many of the different avenues, and by deciding what I did not want to do (e.g., work as a school counselor), I was able to whittle down my choices. It came down to a choice between clinical psychology and marriage and family therapy (MFT). I knew I wanted to be a therapist; however, I was very intrigued by clinical work with those suffering from severe mental disorders. After much research and thought, I finally chose to obtain my degree in MFT, largely because of the degree's broad nature. With this degree I would have the potential to become licensed and could work with a large variety of clients, including families, couples, and even individuals. My main worry in taking this route was that I would not get the experience I had hoped for working with a more clinical population (as opposed to simply working with clients with relational and transitional problems).

I finally chose to attend the University of San Francisco, working on a degree in counseling psychology with an emphasis on MFT. My previous concern about limiting the population(s) I would work with was alleviated when I chose the agency at which I would complete my traineeship. My traineeship is at a substance abuse agency, where many of the clients have a dual diagnosis of substance abuse and another psychological disorder. This setting allows me to deal with a wide range of clients and psychological issues simultaneously in my work.

The following are some tips on choosing a graduate school in the MFT field. Make sure to really research your graduate school. Do not be afraid to ask them questions! Make sure to choose a program where many of the professors have their own private practices. Many professors will use examples from their actual past cases to provide concrete examples in class, which is great, especially in a field that can be very theoretical.

Overall, the MFT path is ideal if you have know you want to work in mental health and have a general idea of what you want to do (e.g., work with couples) but do not want to choose anything too specialized from the start. Once you obtain the degree, you can then decide with which kinds of therapy and/or populations you want to work. Another benefit is that you will always have the option of working in private practice.

GENERAL JOB ACTIVITIES OF PRACTICING PSYCHOLOGISTS

Clinical psychologists and others who work in related helping professions, such as counseling and social work, are employed in many settings, including group practices, hospitals, counseling centers, clinics, schools, universities and colleges, substance abuse facilities, and correctional facilities. Job duties differ depending on the specific helping career and the population being served. Some common job duties may include interviewing clients, giving and scoring diagnostic tests, and maintaining written records regarding clients' cases. Work duties may also include developing treatment plans to assist individuals with personal, family, educational, social, occupational, and other difficulties, depending upon the practitioner's specialty. Treatment plans may consist of behavior modification and/or therapy and may also require coordination with other professionals, including medical doctors. (Note, though, that medical doctors are currently the only professionals who can prescribe medication for mental health disorders in all but a few states.)

Professionals who provide therapy must be very good communicators, good listeners, patient, and responsible. Providing therapy is not as easy as simply getting clients to open up and talk; it involves many skills, especially listening and social skills. Therapy consists of goal-oriented discussions in which therapists ask clients specific questions to learn information that therapists need to provide effective treatment. Therapists actively lead conversations based on their client's therapeutic goals and often attempt to guide clients through their own process of self-exploration and self-realization. Therapists must have the ability to hear about difficult personal situations and circumstances and to react empathetically yet objectively. Professional guidelines in such careers require that professionals do not become emotionally involved in clients' lives.

You may be wondering what the major differences are among those individuals who work under the many practice-related jobs mentioned in this section. The answer is not cut and dry because professional duties may be similar among individuals working in these different professions. In addition, even people working under the same title (e.g., social worker) may fulfill various roles depending on the type of organization in which they work, their work setting, their number of years of experience, and so forth. The following brief career descriptions provide you with a general overview of the major differences among some common job titles related to the practice of psychology.

Clinical Psychologist

Clinical psychologists may work in various settings, including hospitals, private practice, and colleges and universities. Many have specialty areas (or issues) in which they (a) help people cope with a particular disorder or set of disorders (e.g., anxiety, depression, impulse control disorders), (b) combine different treatment approaches or have a preferred method of treatment (e.g., cognitive–behavioral therapy), and (c) focus on working with particular populations (e.g., teens, the elderly). They must hold a license as a "licensed psychologist" in the state in which they practice to work with clients. They provide psychotherapy to pathological populations (people suffering from relatively more serious mental health issues) and are trained in various methods of assessment. They tend to focus on the individual's thoughts, emotions, and behaviors and may take different approaches to changing cognitions and behaviors as a part of treatment. To learn more about what it might be like to work as a clinical psychologist, see Exhibit 7.4.

Counseling Psychologist

Counselors may work in similar settings to those of clinical psychologists and must be licensed psychologists in the state in which they practice. The major difference between counselors and clinical psychologists is that counselors do not work with clients suffering from severe or persistent mental illness. Counselors provide psychotherapy and help individuals develop strengths and adaptive strategies throughout the lifespan. They focus on emotional, social, educational, health, and organizational concerns and may conduct vocational and career counseling or assessment.

Marriage and Family Therapist

Marriage and family therapists must hold a license or have certification to work with clients in the state in which they practice. Although many marriage and family therapists work in private practice, many work in social services agencies, universities, community mental health clinics, prisons, courts, inpatient facilities, and other settings. They treat emotional disorders within the context of the family unit and may meet with several family members for family therapy sessions. They focus on helping resolve relationship problems, resolving communication issues, and guiding clients through transitional crises (e.g., death of a loved one). They diagnose and treat a wide range of clinical problems, including depression, marital problems, and child–parent problems.

School Psychologist

Most school psychologists work in public or private school systems. Most states require school psychologists to hold master's degrees in school psychology and a certification or license (see http://www.nasponline.org/

EXHIBIT 7.4

One Professional's Perspective

Tina Freeland, PhD, Licensed Clinical Psychologist, Private Practice
"A Career in Private Practice"

People often ask, "How do you do this work?" Their question refers to the hours spent listening to others as they pour out their stories of pain, anger, trauma, loss, shame, guilt, and all of the other human emotions that punctuate human life. Aside from the professional satisfaction that my work provides, there is no easy or singular way to explain why one is attracted to the field of clinical psychology or what keeps a clinician practicing for years on end. Most of us who become clinical psychologists have very strong listening skills and are quite curious about human nature. Good psychologists are also empathic, sincere, respectful, and ethical. Individuals must have certain personal qualities to become a competent and successful psychologist, qualities that are deeply rooted in a person and are developed out of personal commitment.

Not all psychologists begin their education in the field of psychology. My own undergraduate degree from University of California, Los Angeles is in English (literature). What better training to become a psychologist can one receive than from the stories and narratives we find in literature? From literature I gained a deep understanding of symbolism, myth, and the human condition. Who can surpass Shakespeare or Dostoevsky in teaching us about tragic decisions and their consequences? What sources beyond our vast library of world literature can better educate us about the extraordinary range and depth of human experience across cultures and ages? Where can we look for more engaging illustrations of family and intergenerational drama than those provided in literature? Students who complete their bachelor's degree in fields as diverse as education, business, biology, and the arts develop an integrated and liberal view of human nature that is central to the practice of clinical psychology.

I completed my doctorate at the University of Southern California, with extensive training in psychological theory and practices, philosophical foundations, research and statistics, as well as a long internship. In the nearly 30 years since, I have worked in private practice, providing psychotherapy to individuals (children, adolescents, and adults), couples, families, and groups. A typical day might include seeing several individual patients experiencing depression, anxiety, and substance abuse, as well as couples and families with relationship difficulties. When a patient first seeks psychotherapy, the psychologist's initial job is to assess the nature of the problem. Most of the time, this assessment occurs through a clinical interview in which the therapist gathers extensive information on the patient's background and history. Sometimes it is also necessary to administer standardized tests to patients to fully define and conceptualize their difficulties.

The actual work of psychotherapy is personal, often painful and uncertain, but ultimately hopeful and rewarding. People usually come to therapy because their lives have become difficult, dysfunctional, and stuck, and they do not know how to repair the problems on their own. Sometimes difficulties in the present have powerful roots in the past, and patterns of behavior are anchored to perceptions and experiences from another period in life. At other times, individuals make decisions based on their best judgment and intentions but lack resources to explore better options. Regardless of the source of the problem, my work is to assess, conceptualize, and create a treatment path for recovery. The general field of psychology has many models that clinicians draw from in developing a treatment plan. Most experienced clinical psychologists, including myself, integrate methods and strategies from these multiple approaches to meet the unique needs of each patient.

Some of the most intense work I have done as a clinical psychologist was completed in hospital settings. When patients become so ill that they cannot safely function independently in their daily lives, hospitalization becomes necessary. Understanding severe mental illness, including schizophrenia, bipolar disorder, major depression, and suicidal intentions, as well as

EXHIBIT 7.4 *(Continued)*

dementia and delusional disorders, has given me a lasting regard for the struggle and bravery of individuals who must be treated in the safety of a hospital setting. Clinical psychologists are able to acquire hospital privileges that allow them to admit, assess, and treat these individuals and to work with the families who must learn how to understand and support the mentally ill.

In both private practice and inpatient work, clinical psychologists work closely with other professionals, particularly psychiatrists and primary care physicians. Because psychologists are not licensed to dispense medications (unless they have completed medical school), they collaborate with medical doctors to discuss the medication options that might help certain patients. I see my patients regularly, usually at least once a week, and am able to provide important clinical information to prescribing doctors who will consider my input in selecting medications. Medical doctors see their patients far less frequently (sometimes only every 2 to 3 months) and, therefore, rely on my observations and communication about the patients we treat in common. I have a comprehensive understanding of psychopharmacology that is necessary in this collaboration with medical doctors.

The work of clinical psychologists requires ongoing learning, professional development, and personal growth. Clinical psychologists must complete a certain number of continuing education hours for their license to be renewed every 2 years. These educational requirements afford clinical psychologists the opportunity to refresh their skills and to acquire new specialized training in areas of interest. Animal-assisted therapy is one of my areas of personal interest, and, over the past 5 years, I have learned to use my dog in sessions for specific therapeutic purposes. Moses (a rescued Rhodesian Ridgeback) and I are trained and certified as "Pet Partners" through the Delta Society so that we can work together in helping others feel, talk, take comfort, and heal. I am also very drawn to the new neurobiological research on trauma and attachment, which provides hopeful applications in the field.

Finally, returning to the original question, we ask ourselves how one does the work of clinical psychology, year after year, without suffering burn out, overidentification with illness, physical distress due to emotional distress, or boredom. I train graduate students who are completing their internship requirements to become licensed clinical psychologists, and this question is asked over and over. Self-care is an essential aspect of being a successful psychotherapist who is able to sustain the clinical work over many years. Being mindful of one's emotional and physical state is critical, as is finding individual ways of maintaining one's personal health. Yoga, meditation and spiritual experiences, exercise, social engagement, sports and hobbies, recreation, and vacations are examples of self-care activities that clinical psychologists turn to in order to keep themselves in good health. Last, psychologists often consult with their own psychotherapists to address the personal issues that arise in their lives as well as those that arise as a consequence of their work.

certification/state_info_list.aspx for a list of each state's licensing requirements). School psychologists work with students, parents, teachers, and school administrators to address students' social and behavioral problems and to ensure that students can learn in a safe and appropriate environment. They often conduct several types of psychological and educational assessments to identify the source of students' problems. They consult with parents and teachers, educate parents and teachers about behavioral management techniques, educate parents regarding parent–child communication, advise school administrators regarding disciplinary actions, refer students and families to counseling services, and so on. Read one professional's perspective in Exhibit 7.5 to learn more about what it might be like to be a school psychologist.

EXHIBIT 7.5

One Professional's Perspective

Simone Gunderson, MA, School Psychologist, Capistrano Unified School District
"A Career as a School Psychologist"

I have always had a passion for children and have wanted to work in a career that allowed me to make a difference for them. During my undergraduate studies, I began researching careers that involved working in the educational system and the opportunity to work directly with students. While doing this research, I discovered the field of school psychology. I chose the field of school psychology for both the challenge and the positive impact I can have on a child's education.

I discovered that a school psychologist typically works within a school setting, providing services to students from the preschool through the secondary level. They collaborate with teachers, parents, and professionals to determine the best learning environment for students. Their duties typically include conducting educational evaluations to determine the appropriate placement of students. Additionally, they counsel students, provide parent and teacher consultations, and are sought after as a resource for student interventions.

After completing my bachelor's degree from the University of California, Irvine, I began working on my graduate degree at Azusa Pacific University in Southern California. This program combined both a master of arts in educational psychology and a Pupil Personnel Services Credential in school psychology. A Pupil Personnel Services Credential is required to practice as a school psychologist in the state of California. The graduate program consisted of a minimum of 60 graduate units, which included a 1,200-hr internship. The graduate course of study focused on counseling, academic and behavioral interventions, psychoeducational assessments, research, and evaluation.

Prior to completing my graduate degree, I held a variety of jobs working with students with disabilities. This kind of experience can be very valuable when entering the field of school psychology. I worked as an intensive behavioral intervention instructor for preschool-age students with moderate to severe autism. This position was especially helpful gaining experience working with the growing number of students with autism in our school system.

Currently, I work for Capistrano Unified School District as a full-time school psychologist. I am positioned at both a middle school and an elementary school. As a school psychologist, I have many duties, including conducting psychoeducational evaluations on students and providing the resulting information to parents and staff regarding the appropriate placement of students. These evaluations may include intelligence testing, academic evaluations, and determinations of how a student is functioning both socially and emotionally. Counseling students on various issues such as school success, behavior, and emotional issues is also an important part of my job. Most school psychologists also serve on their school's crisis management team to provide support and consultation in the event of a school crisis. Additionally, as a member of the school's intervention team, I participate in meetings regarding particular students who are struggling.

The field of school psychology can be very rewarding. School psychologists work in collaboration with teachers, parents, and administrators to promote student success. There seems to be a steady need for professionals in the field of school psychology. If working with children and helping them see their true potential seems interesting, a career in school psychology may be for you.

Social Worker

Most social workers work in either clinical settings similar to those of clinical psychologists or in community practice. Social workers in clinical practice can work with clients using various therapeutic tools, such as psychotherapy, individual or group counseling, crisis intervention, case management, substance abuse counseling, and hospice counseling. Social workers who work in community practice tend to focus on community organizing, policy analysis, and management in human services. They may work for nonprofit organizations, government agencies, political agencies, or in similar settings. Most states require social workers to have a license as a social worker, and a master's degree is required for clinical practice.

Psychiatrist

Psychiatrists are medical doctors who work in medical settings or private practice settings. Because of their medical training, psychiatrists are the only mental health practitioners who can prescribe medication in most states (Louisiana and New Mexico currently allow some psychologists limited prescribing privileges, and other states have been attempting to pass the same legislation without success). The majority of psychiatrists' time with patients is usually spent addressing medication and medication management. Psychiatrists tend to refer patients to clinical psychologists who specialize in providing patients with psychotherapy and/or behavioral treatment.

SELF ASSESSMENT: IS PRACTICE RIGHT FOR YOU?

Here are some questions that you can ask yourself to determine whether you might be well suited for a career in practicing psychology.

- Do I have an appreciation for others' points of view?
- Am I sensitive to individual differences in cultures, values, and religion?
- Do I relate well to people interpersonally?
- Do I have extremely high levels of patience?
- Would I enjoy working with others for the majority of the day?
- Do I have a strong interest in the human mind?
- Can I accept the fact that I cannot "cure" everyone?
- Can I deal with people relying on me emotionally?
- Can I separate my professional life from private life very well (i.e., can I leave the day's job at work when I go home)?
- Am I willing to deal with the business side of practice, such as marketing and dealing with insurance claims, managed care, paperwork, and record keeping?
- Am I willing to devote 5 or more years to graduate study?

- Is helping others personally rewarding to me?
- Am I motivated to help others?

If you answered "yes" to many or most of these questions, then you may be well suited for a career in helping others and the practice of psychology.

MY PROACTIVE PLAN EXERCISES

1. If I were to become a psychology professor, would I prefer to work at a teaching-oriented college or research-oriented institution? Why?
2. In completing the self-assessment entitled, "Is Research Right for You?" did I find myself answering "yes" or "no" to questions more often? How might I interpret the results of my self-assessment?
3. In completing the self-assessment entitled, "Is Research Right for You?" which statement did I agree with most strongly? Why?
4. In completing the self-assessment entitled, "Is Research Right for You?" which statement did I disagree with most strongly? Why?
5. In reading this chapter, what information about the practice of psychology stood out the most to me? Why did this information stand out or surprise me?
6. Which practice-related career presented in this chapter seems most interesting to me? Why?
7. If I were to practice psychology in the future, with which population(s) (e.g., children, typical adults, prison inmates, the elderly) do I think I would prefer to work? Why?
8. If I were to practice psychology in the future, in which potential work settings (e.g., university or college, hospital, counseling center, private practice, correctional facility) do I think I would prefer to work? In which would I least prefer to work? Why do I feel this way?
9. In completing the self-assessment entitled, "Is Practice Right for You?" did I find myself answering "yes" or "no" to questions more often? How might I interpret the results of my self-assessment?
10. In completing the self-assessment entitled, "Is Practice Right for You?" which statement did I agree with most strongly? Why?
11. In completing the self-assessment entitled, "Is Practice Right for You?" which statement did I disagree with most strongly? Why?

Appendix A
Scholarly Journals in Major
Subdisciplines of Psychology

General psychology:
American Behavioral Scientist
American Psychologist
Annual Review of Psychology
Canadian Journal of Behavioural Science
Current Directions in Psychological Science
International Journal of Psychology
Journal of Applied Psychology
Journal of Experimental Psychology
Psychological Bulletin
Psychological Review
Psychological Science

Behavior and applied behavioral analysis:
Animal Learning and Behavior
Behavioral Processes
Journal of Applied Behavioral Analysis
Journal of Early and Intensive Behavioral Intervention
Journal of Early Intervention
Journal of the Experimental Analysis of Behavior

Biological psychology:
Behavioral Neuroscience
Biological Psychology
Biofeedback

Brain and Behavior
Canadian Journal of Behavioural Science
Journal of Biological Psychology
Journal of Comparative Psychology
Journal of Experimental Psychology: Animal Behavior Processes
Journal of Neuroscience
Nature Neuroscience
Neuron

Clinical psychology:
American Journal of Psychoanalysis
American Journal of Psychotherapy
American Journal on Addictions
American Psychoanalyst
Clinical Psychology and Psychotherapy
Clinical Psychology Review
Journal of Abnormal Psychology
Journal of Clinical Child Psychology
Journal of Clinical Psychology
Journal of Counseling Psychology
Psychotherapy & Psychosomatics
Psychoanalytic Psychology
Psychological Assessment
Psychotherapy: Therapy, Research, Practice, and Policy

Cognitive psychology:
Cognitive Science
Journal of Experimental Psychology: Human Perception and Performance
Journal of Memory and Cognition
Journal of Memory and Language
Psychonomic Bulletin & Review
International Journal of Psycholinguistics
Journal of Cognitive Neuroscience
Language and Cognitive Processes

Developmental psychology:
Child Development
Cognitive Development
Developmental Psychology
Social Development
Journal of Experimental Child Psychology
Psychology and Aging

Health psychology:
Experimental and Clinical Psychopharmacology
Families, Systems, & Health
Health Psychology
International Journal of Stress Management

Neuropsychology
Psychology of Addictive Behaviors
Rehabilitation Psychology

Industrial–organizational psychology:
Group Dynamics: Theory, Research, and Practice
Group Facilitation: A Research and Applications Journal
Group Processes & Intergroup Relations
Journal of Economic Psychology
Journal of Organizational Behavior
Journal of Vocational Behavior
Organizational Behavior and Human Decision Processes
Organizational Research Methods
Personnel Psychology
Small Group Research

Judgment and decision making:
Acta Psychologica
Judgment and Decision Making
Journal of Behavioral Decision Making
Journal of Forecasting
Journal of Heuristics
Journal of Risk and Uncertainty
Risk, Decision and Policy
Theory and Decision
Thinking and Reasoning

Sensation and perception:
Investigative Ophthalmology & Visual Science
Journal of Chemical Senses
Journal of Vision
Perception
Perception and Psychophysics
Vision Research
Visual Neuroscience

Social psychology:
Basic and Applied Social Psychology
Current Research in Social Psychology
Journal of Applied Social Psychology
Journal of Community and Applied Social Psychology
Journal of Experimental Social Psychology
Journal of Personality and Social Psychology
Journal of Social Psychology
Personality and Social Psychology Bulletin and Review
Social Cognition
Social Issues and Policy Review
Social Psychology Quarterly

Appendix B
Major Organizations Hosting Annual Psychology Research Conferences in the United States

American Psychological Association (http://www.apa.org)

Association for Behavioral Analysis International (http://www.abainternational.org)

Association for Psychological Science (http://www.psychologicalscience.org)

Eastern Psychological Association (http://www.easternpsychological.org)

Midwestern Psychological Association (http://www.midwesternpsych.org)

New England Psychological Association (http://www.nepa-info.org)

Psi Chi (http://www.psichi.org/conventions)

Rocky Mountain Psychological Association (http://www.rockymountainpsych.org)

Society for Research in Child Development (http://www.srcd.org)

Society for Neuroscience (http://www.sfn.org)

Southeastern Psychological Association (http://www.sepaonline.com)

Southwestern Psychological Association (http://www.swpsych.org)

Western Psychological Association (http://www.westernpsych.org)

References

American Psychological Association. (2007). *Getting in: A step-by-step plan for gaining admission to graduate school in psychology.* Washington, DC: Author.

American Psychological Association. (2009). *Graduate study in psychology 2010.* Washington, DC: Author.

American Psychological Association Center for Workforce Studies. (2008a). *Frequently asked questions.* Retrieved from http://research.apa.org/faq.html#II3

American Psychological Association Center for Workforce Studies. (2008b). *Occupational characteristics of baccalaureate degree recipients in psychology: 1999.* Retrieved from http://research.apa.org/baccalaureate03.html

American Psychological Association Center for Workforce Studies. (2008c). *Primary and secondary work Activities of baccalaureate degree recipients: 1999.* Retrieved from http://research.apa.org/baccalaureate04.html

American Psychological Association Center for Workforce Studies. (2009). [Data from the 2008 APA directory, compiled by the Center for Workforce Studies]. Unpublished data.

American Psychological Association Education Directorate. (2008). *Graduate education: Frequently asked questions.* Retrieved from http://www.apa.org/ed/graduate/faqs.html#time

American Psychological Association. (2010). *Careers in Psychology.* Retrieved from http://www.apa.org/careers/resources/guides/careers.aspx

Appleby, D. (1997). *The handbook of psychology.* New York, NY: Longman.

Buskist, W., & Burke, C. (2007). *Preparing for graduate study in psychology: 101 questions and answers* (2nd ed.). Malden, MA: Blackwell.

Costa, P. T., & McCrae, R. R. (1992). Normal personality assessment in clinical practice: The NEO Personality Inventory. *Psychological Assessment, 4,* 5–13.

Crosby, O. (2000–2001). Degrees to dollars: Earnings of college graduates in 1998. *Occupational Outlook Quarterly, 44*(4), 30–38.

DeGalan, J., & Lambert, S. (1995). *Great jobs for psychology majors.* Lincolnwood, IL: VGM Career Horizons.

Edwards, J., & Smith, K. (1988). What skills and knowledge do potential employers value in baccalaureate psychologists? In P. J. Woods (Ed.), *Is psychology for them? A guide to undergraduate advising* (pp. 102–111). Washington, DC: American Psychological Association.

Gaddy, C. D., Charlot-Swilley, D., Nelson, P. D., & Reich, J. N. (1995). Selected outcomes of accredited programs. *Professional Psychology: Research and Practice, 26,* 507–513.

Harton, H. C., & Lyons, P. C. (2003). Gender, empathy, and the choice of the psychology major. *Teaching of Psychology, 30,* 19–24.

John, O. P., & Srivastava, S. (1999). The Big Five Trait taxonomy: History, measurement, and theoretical perspectives. In L. A. Pervin & O. P. John (Eds.), *Handbook of personality: Theory and research* (2nd ed., pp. 102–138). New York, NY: Guilford.

Kracen, A. C., & Wallace, I. G. (Eds.). (2008). *Applying to graduate school in psychology: Advice from successful students and prominent psychologists.* Washington, DC: American Psychological Association.

Kressel, N. J. (1990). Job and degree satisfaction among social science graduates. *Teaching of Psychology, 17,* 222–227.

Kruger, D. J., & Zechmeister, E. B. (2001). A skills–experience inventory for the undergraduate psychology major. *Teaching of Psychology, 28,* 249–253.

Kuther, T. L. (2003). *The psychology major's handbook.* Pacific Grove, CA: Thomson/Wadsworth.

Landrum, R. E. (2009). *Finding jobs with a psychology bachelor's degree: Expert advice for launching your career.* Washington, DC: American Psychological Association.

Landrum, R. E., & Davis, S. F. (2003). *The psychology major: Career options and strategies for success* (2nd ed.). Upper Saddle River, NJ: Prentice-Hall.

Lock, R. (1988). A history of practical work in school science and its assessment, 1860–1986. *School Science Review, 70,* 115–119.

Lunneborg, P. W., & Wilson, V. M. (1985). Would you major in psychology again? *Teaching of Psychology, 12,* 17–20.

Marrs, H., Barb, M. R., & Ruggiero, J. C. (2007). Self-reported influences on psychology major choice and personality. *Individual Differences Research, 5,* 289–299.

Meeker, F., Fox, D., & Whitley, B. E. (1994). Predictors of academic success in the undergraduate psychology major. *Teaching of Psychology, 21,* 238–241.

National Center for Education Statistics. (2008a). *Bachelor's degrees conferred by degree-granting institutions, by field of study: Selected years, 1970–71 through 2006–07.* Retrieved from http://www.nces.ed.gov/programs/digest/d08/tables/dt08_271.asp

National Center for Education Statistics. (2008b). *Enrollment in post-secondary education, by student level, type of institution, age, and major field of study: 2003–04.* Retrieved from http://www.nces.ed.gov/programs/digest/d08/tables/dt08_232.asp

National Science Foundation. (2006). *Special report: U.S. doctorates in the 20th century.* Retrieved from http://www.nsf.gov/statistics/nsf06319/

National Science Foundation. (2008a). *An overview of science, engineering, and health graduates: 2006.* Retrieved from http://www.nsf.gov/statistics/infbrief/nsf08304/

National Science Foundation. (2008b). Survey of doctorate recipients. Retrieved from http://www.nsf.gov/statistics/srvydoctoratework/

Norcross, J. C., & Castle, P. H. (2002). Appreciating the PsyD: The facts. *Eye on Psi Chi, 7*(1), 22–26.

Norcross, J. C., Sayette, M. A., & Mayne, T. J. (2008). *Insider's guide to graduate programs in clinical and counseling psychology.* New York, NY: Guilford.

Pryor, J. H., Hurtado, S., Saenz, V. B., Lindhom, J. A., Korn, W. S., & Mahoney, K. M. (2005). *The American freshman: National norms for fall 2005.* Los Angeles: University of California, Los Angeles, Higher Education Research Institute.

Rajecki, D. W. (2005). *Master list of job titles.* Retrieved from http://dwrajecki.com/job-titles.htm

Rajecki, D. W. (2008). Job lists for entry-level psychology baccalaureates: Occupational recommendations that mismatch qualifications. *Teaching of Psychology, 35,* 33–37.

Roberson, L. (1990). Prediction of job satisfaction from characteristics of personal work goals. *Journal of Organizational Behavior, 11,* 29–41.

Schultheiss, D. E. P. (2008). *Psychology as a major: Is it right for me and what can I do with my degree?* Washington, DC: American Psychological Association.

Silvia, P. J., Delaney, P. F., & Marcovitch, S. (2009). *What psychology majors could (and should) be doing: An informal guide to research experience and professional skills.* Washington, DC: American Psychological Association.

Sternberg, R. J. (2007). *Career paths in psychology: Where your degree can take you* (2nd ed.). Washington, DC: American Psychological Association.

Stringer, T. T. (2000–2001). Four years after graduation: The class of 1993. *Occupational Outlook Quarterly, 44*(4), 16–29.

Stroup, C. M., & Benjamin, L. T. J. (1982). Graduate study in psychology 1970–1979. *American Psychologist, 37,* 1186–1202.

U.S. Bureau of Labor Statistics. (2000). *Number of jobs held, labor market activity, and earnings growth over two decades: Results from a longitudinal survey (NLSY79 Round 18).* Retrieved from http://www.bls.gov/nls/y79r22jobsbyage.pdf

U.S. Bureau of Labor Statistics. (2006). *Occupational outlook handbook.* Washington, DC: U.S. Government Printing Office.

Index

About the Authors

Amira Rezec Wegenek, PhD, is a professor of psychology at Saddleback College in California. Dr. Wegenek has taught, mentored, and advised undergraduates at the university and college level for over a decade. She has received numerous awards for teaching and leadership, including the Psi Beta National Honor Society in Psychology National "Rising Star" Award for mentoring undergraduates in scholarship, research, and service. Her students have won national recognition for their research and service activities as well. Her publications span the areas of sensation and perception, cognitive psychology, and teaching of psychology and include a student-centered psychology laboratory manual. She is currently an active member of the Society for the Teaching of Psychology and conducts research related to student retention and success.

William Buskist, PhD, is a Distinguished Professor in the Teaching of Psychology at Auburn University and a faculty fellow at Auburn's Biggio Center for the Enhancement of Teaching and Learning. In his 27 years at Auburn University, he has taught over 32,000 undergraduates, mostly in large sections of introductory psychology. He served as the section editor for "The Generalist's Corner" section of *Teaching of Psychology* and is currently a member of the National Institute on the Teaching of Psychology Planning Committee. Together with Steve Davis, he has edited two volumes on the teaching of psychology: *The Teaching of Psychology: Essays in Honor of Wilbert J. McKeachie and Charles L. Brewer* and *The Handbook of the Teaching of Psychology*. In addition, together with Barry Perlman and Lee McCann, he has edited *Voices of Experience: Memorable Talks From the National Institute on the Teaching of Psychology*. He has also coedited several electronic books for the Society of the Teaching of Psychology (http://teachpsych.org/resources/e-books/e-books.php). Currently, along with Doug Bernstein, he is the coeditor of the *Teaching Psychology Science* series, which focuses on providing advice and tips for teaching specific courses in psychology (e.g., introductory psychology, developmental psychology, research methods, statistics). He has published over 30 books and articles on the teaching of psychology. In 2005, he was a co-recipient (with Leanne Lamke) of Auburn University's highest teaching honor, The Gerald and Emily Leischuck Presidential Award for Excellence in Teaching. He was also the American Psychological Association's (APA's) 2005 Harry Kirke Wolfe lecturer and the recipient of the 2000 Robert S. Daniel Teaching Excellence Award from the Society of the Teaching of Psychology. In 2009, he received the American Psychological Foundation's Charles L. Brewer Distinguished Teaching of Psychology Award and APA Division 25's (Behavior Analysis) Fred S. Keller Behavioral Education Award. He is a fellow of APA Divisions 1 (General Psychology), 2 (Society for the Teaching of Psychology), and 52 (International Psychology). He also served as president of the Society for the Teaching of Psychology in 2007. Six of his graduate students have been honored with national teaching awards.